POINT
COUNTERPOINT

Capital
Punishment

POINT ||||////
||||||| COUNTERPOINT

Capital Punishment
Freedom of Speech
Gun Control
Mental Health Reform
The Right to Privacy
Trial of Juveniles as Adults

Capital Punishment

Alan Marzilli

SERIES CONSULTING EDITOR
Alan Marzilli, M.A., J.D.

CHELSEA HOUSE
PUBLISHERS
A Haights Cross Communications Company

Philadelphia

This book is intended to serve only as a general introduction to the political and legal issues surrounding capital punishment. It is not intended as legal advice. If you have a legal problem, you should consult a licensed attorney who is familiar with the laws and procedures of your jurisdiction.

CHELSEA HOUSE PUBLISHERS

VP, New Product Development Sally Cheney
Director of Production Kim Shinners
Creative Manager Takeshi Takahashi
Manufacturing Manager Diann Grasse

Staff for CAPITAL PUNISHMENT

Editor Patrick M.N. Stone
Production Editor Jaimie Winkler
Photo Editor Sarah Bloom
Series and Cover Designer Keith Trego
Layout 21st Century Publishing and Communications, Inc.

Library of Congress Cataloging-in-Publication Data

Marzilli, Alan.
   Capital punishment / Alan Marzilli.
       p. cm.—(Point-counterpoint)
Includes index.
   ISBN 0-7910-7369-6 HC   0-7910-7505-2 PB
   1. Capital punishment—Juvenile literature. I Title. II Series: Point-counterpoint
(Philadelphia, Pa.)
HV8694 .M327 2002
364.66—dc21

                                                        2002015608

11/05

||||||||CONTENTS

Introduction
Alan Marzilli, M.A., J.D.
Durham, North Carolina

The debates presented in POINT/COUNTERPOINT are among the most interesting and controversial in contemporary American society, but studying them is more than an academic activity. They affect every citizen; they are the issues that today's leaders debate and tomorrow's will decide. The reader may one day play a central role in resolving them.

Why study both sides of the debate? It's possible that the reader will not yet have formed any opinion at all on the subject of this volume—but this is unlikely. It is more likely that the reader will already hold an opinion, probably a strong one, and very probably one formed without full exposure to the arguments of the other side. It is rare to hear an argument presented in a balanced way, and it is easy to form an opinion on too little information; these books will help to fill in the informational gaps that can never be avoided. More important, though, is the practical function of the series: Skillful argumentation requires a thorough knowledge of *both* sides—though there are seldom only two, and only by knowing what an opponent is likely to assert can one form an articulate response.

Perhaps more important is that listening to the other side sometimes helps one to see an opponent's arguments in a more human way. For example, Sister Helen Prejean, one of the nation's most visible opponents of capital punishment, has been deeply affected by her interactions with the families of murder victims. Seeing the families' grief and pain, she understands much better why people support the death penalty, and she is able to carry out her advocacy with a greater sensitivity to the needs and beliefs of those who do not agree with her. Her relativism, in turn, lends credibility to her work. Dismissing the other side of the argument as totally without merit can be too easy—it is far more useful to understand the nature of the controversy and the reasons *why* the issue defies resolution.

The most controversial issues of all are often those that center on a constitutional right. The Bill of Rights—the first ten amendments to the U.S. Constitution—spells out some of the most fundamental rights that distinguish the governmental system of the United States from those that allow fewer (or other) freedoms. But the sparsely worded document is open to interpretation, and clauses of only a few words are often at the heart of national debates. The Bill of Rights was meant to protect individual liberties; but the needs of some individuals clash with those of society as a whole, and when this happens someone has to decide where to draw the line. Thus the Constitution becomes a battleground between the rights of individuals to do as they please and the responsibility of the government to protect its citizens. The First Amendment's guarantee of "freedom of speech," for example, leads to a number of difficult questions. Some forms of expression, such as burning an American flag, lead to public outrage—but nevertheless are said to be protected by the First Amendment. Other types of expression that most people find objectionable, such as sexually explicit material involving children, are not protected because they are considered harmful. The question is not only where to draw the line, but how to do this without infringing on the personal liberties on which the United States was built.

The Bill of Rights raises many other questions about individual rights and the societal "good." Is a prayer before a high school football game an "establishment of religion" prohibited by the First Amendment? Does the Second Amendment's promise of "the right to bear arms" include concealed handguns? Is stopping and frisking someone standing on a corner known to be frequented by drug dealers a form of "unreasonable search and seizure" in violation of the Fourth Amendment? Although the nine-member U.S. Supreme Court has the ultimate authority in interpreting the Constitution, its answers do not always satisfy the public. When a group of nine people—sometimes by a five-to-four vote—makes a decision that affects the lives of hundreds of millions, public outcry can be expected. And the composition of the Court does change over time, so even a landmark decision is not guaranteed to stand forever. The limits of constitutional protection are always in flux.

These issues make headlines, divide courts, and decide elections. They are the questions most worthy of national debate, and this series aims to cover them as thoroughly as possible. Each volume sets out some of the key arguments surrounding a particular issue, even some views that most people consider extreme or radical—but presents a balanced perspective on the issue. Excerpts from the relevant laws and judicial opinions and references to central concepts, source material, and advocacy groups help the reader to explore the issues even further and to read "the letter of the law" just as the legislatures and the courts have established it.

It may seem that some debates—such as those over capital punishment and abortion, debates with a strong moral component—will never be resolved. But American history offers numerous examples of controversies that once seemed insurmountable but now are effectively settled, even if only on the surface. Abolitionists met with widespread resistance to their efforts to end slavery, and the controversy over that issue threatened to cleave the nation in two; but today public debate over the merits of slavery would be unthinkable, though racial inequalities still plague the nation. Similarly unthinkable at one time was suffrage for women and minorities, but this is now a matter of course. Distributing information about contraception once was a crime. Societies change, and attitudes change, and new questions of social justice are raised constantly while the old ones fade into irrelevancy.

Whatever the root of the controversy, the books in POINT/ COUNTERPOINT seek to explain to the reader the origins of the debate, the current state of the law, and the arguments on both sides. The goal of the series is to inform the reader about the issues facing not only American politicians, but all of the nation's citizens, and to encourage the reader to become more actively involved in resolving these debates, as a voter, a concerned citizen, a journalist, an activist, or an elected official. Democracy is based on education, and every voice counts—so every opinion must be an informed one.

This volume examines the controversy over capital punishment, a debate that has divided courts and has been the center of political elections, including presidential elections. The death penalty has a long history, but today the United States' continued use of capital punishment sets it apart from other Western democracies, in a league with some of the world's most oppressive regimes. Still, a majority of Americans support capital punishment.

While moral and religious questions pervade the debate, a number of legal and sociological questions are also relevant: Does the death penalty deter would-be criminals? Should executions be streamlined, or should safeguards cause the court process to take years or decades? Does the death penalty discriminate against the poor and minorities? These and other questions keep the death penalty debate at the forefront of the American consciousness year after year.

What Is Capital Punishment?

S ome of today's greatest moral and legal questions concern capital punishment. Should the government have the power to sentence convicted criminals to death? Throughout history, societies have punished criminals by executing them, but today many nations have abolished the death penalty. In the United States, however, the federal government and many of the states continue to sentence people to death.

A Brief History of Capital Punishment

In ancient times, methods of execution were particularly bloody. In addition to crucifixion, the Bible mentions punishments such as being put to death by a crowd of people throwing stones. The death penalty was given for crimes that would be considered minor, or not crimes at all, by today's standards. For centuries—throughout the Middle Ages and the Renaissance—little changed. According to Harry Henderson:

> Death was the standard penalty for major crimes across Europe. The methods of execution used frequently were cruel and barbaric by modern standards, often involving some form of torture. The condemned were subject to such ordeals as burning at the stake, being broken on a wheel, or being crushed under heavy stones.[1]

The first significant effort to make executions more humane occurred during the French Revolution of 1789. Prior to the Revolution, members of the aristocracy were executed swiftly by sword. By contrast, peasants and laborers were executed by the slow, torturous methods common at the time. Physician Joseph-Ignace Guillotin proposed to the French Assembly that, in the interest of fairness and equity upon which the Revolution was based, like crimes should be punished with like penalties, and all people put to death should be punished by the same method. He suggested the use of a machine that would behead a condemned person by means of a heavy blade that dropped swiftly onto the back of the neck. This device, eventually called a *guillotine*, was designed to end a person's life quickly rather than through prolonged torture. The king and queen of France were eventually executed by guillotine when the Revolution overthrew the monarchy.

Do you support the death penalty?

What ideas are at the base of your opinion, and where did these ideas come from?

Should everyone feel as you do?

Today, like most European countries, France has abolished the death penalty. In fact, among Western industrialized nations, the United States alone still allows its citizens to be sentenced to death. For a brief period of time, from 1972 to 1977, there were no executions in the United States; this was a result of the Supreme Court's decision in *Furman v. Georgia* (1972), which

The guillotine, a product of Enlightenment science that was widely used during the French Revolution, was the first attempt at humane execution. In the United States today, the most common methods of execution are lethal injection and electrocution, though a few states still employ hanging or the firing squad.

held that the death penalty was unconstitutional because states had no clear-cut standards by which to administer it. Similar crimes often drew very different sentences, and minorities were much more likely to be sentenced to death than Caucasians were. The Court based its decision on the Eighth Amendment: "Excessive bail shall not be required, nor excessive fines imposed, nor cruel and unusual punishment inflicted."

However, the Court's decision in *Gregg v. Georgia* (1976) upheld revised death penalty statutes that gave jurors specific guidance on when to sentence a convicted criminal to death. Complying with *Gregg*, each state that carries the death penalty has a list of "capital offenses" for which the death penalty may be given. Examples include murders that were particularly brutal; murders with multiple victims; murders during the commission of another felony, such as a bank robbery; murders of police officers; and murders for hire.

Since Gary Gilmore was executed by a Utah firing squad in 1977, several hundred more people have been executed in the United States. Over two thirds of the states allow capital punishment, and a variety of methods are used, including the firing squad, in which a number of people fire rifles simultaneously at the condemned person; hanging by the neck with rope; and the gas chamber, which suffocates the condemned person with poisonous gas. For years, the most common method of execution was electrocution using the electric chair, which kills through a series of high-voltage shocks.

> **Is there a humane way to take a life?**
>
> **Why is "humaneness" relevant or irrelevant?**

Today, however, most executions in the United States are by lethal injection of a series of chemicals. The first is an anesthetic, which is used—as with surgery—to prevent pain; however, because an unusually high amount of anesthetic is used for a lethal injection, the anesthetic in itself can be fatal. Next, a chemical is injected to paralyze the lungs and diaphragm, to make breathing impossible. In some states, a third chemical

Method of execution, by State, 2000

Lethal injection		Electrocution	Lethal gas	Hanging	Firing squad
Arizona[a,b]	Nevada	Alabama	Arizona[a,b]	Delaware[a,c]	Idaho[a]
Arkansas[a,d]	New Hampshire[a]	Arkansas[a,d]	California[a]	New Hampshire[a,e]	Oklahoma[f]
California[a]	New Jersey	Florida[a]	Missouri[a]	Washington[a]	Utah[a]
Colorado	New Mexico	Georgia[a,g]	Wyoming[a,h]		
Connecticut	New York	Kentucky[a,i]			
Delaware[a,c]	North Carolina	Nebraska			
Florida[a]	Ohio[a]	Ohio[a]			
Georgia[a,g]	Oklahoma[a]	Oklahoma[f]			
Idaho[a]	Oregon	South Carolina[a]			
Illinois	Pennsylvania	Tennessee[a,j]			
Indiana	South Carolina[a]	Virginia[a]			
Kansas	South Dakota				
Kentucky[a,i]	Tennessee[a,j]				
Louisiana	Texas				
Maryland	Utah[a]				
Mississippi	Virginia[a]				
Missouri[a]	Washington[a]				
Montana	Wyoming[a]				

Note: The method of execution of Federal prisoners is lethal injection, pursuant to 28 CFR, Part 26. For offenses under the Violent Crime Control and Law Enforcement Act of 1994, the method is that of the State in which the conviction took place, pursuant to 18 U.S.C. 3596.
[a]Authorizes 2 methods of execution.
[b]Arizona authorizes lethal injection for persons whose capital sentence was received after 11/15/92; for those sentenced before that date, the condemned may select lethal injection or lethal gas.
[c]Delaware authorizes lethal injection for those whose capital offense occurred after 6/13/86; for those whose offense occurred before that date, the condemned may select lethal injection or hanging.
[d]Arkansas authorizes lethal injection for those whose capital offense occurred on or after 7/4/83; for those whose offense occurred before that date, the condemned may select lethal injection or electrocution.
[e]New Hampshire authorizes hanging only if lethal injection cannot be given.
[f]Oklahoma authorizes electrocution if lethal injection is ever held to be unconstitutional, and firing squad if both lethal injection and electrocution are held unconstitutional.
[g]Georgia authorizes lethal injection for those whose capital offense occurred on or after 5/1/2000; those whose offense occurred before that date are subject to electrocution.
[h]Wyoming authorizes lethal gas if lethal injection is ever held to be unconstitutional.
[i]Kentucky authorizes lethal injection for persons whose capital sentence was received on or after 3/31/98; for those sentenced before that date, the condemned may select lethal injection or electrocution.
[j]Tennessee authorizes lethal injection for those whose capital offense occurred after 12/31/98; those whose offense occurred before that date may select electrocution.

injection is used to cause the heart to stop beating.

Many national and international organizations are working to abolish the death penalty in the United States, but a majority of Americans support the death penalty. As a result, capital punishment is often an important issue in local, state, and national elections. The power of capital punishment as a campaign issue is illustrated by the 1988 presidential election. According to public opinion polls, Republican Vice President George Bush was trailing Democrat Michael Dukakis, Governor of Massachusetts. However, the Bush campaign turned around, thanks in large part to the infamous "Willie Horton" television ads.

Willie Horton was a convicted murderer, but under a Massachusetts program while Dukakis was governor, Horton was temporarily released from prison. During his release, he raped and brutally murdered a woman. Bush, who supported the death penalty, used the ads to attack Dukakis, who was opposed to the death penalty and whom Bush characterized as being soft on crime. Although many thought that the commercials showing a mug shot of Horton—who was black—had racist overtones, the ads were effective in helping Bush to win the election.

The Execution of Robert Willie

While death penalty opponents might be in the minority, many "abolitionists" are very dedicated to the cause. Sister Helen Prejean is one of those people who think that capital punishment is wrong, no matter how heinous the crime. A Catholic nun from Louisiana, she became a vocal opponent of the death penalty while serving as a spiritual advisor to death row inmates. At the same time, she also reached out to the victims' families.

If ever a person could test the strength of Prejean's beliefs, it was Robert Willie, whose crimes were particularly brutal. He had murdered a drug dealer by drowning him. In the spring of 1980, he and another man had raped and killed a young woman, stabbing her 17 times and cutting off several of her fingers as she tried to defend herself. Days later, the pair had kidnapped a young couple and driven them to Alabama, where the two criminals had raped the woman and then tied her boyfriend to a tree and shot him, leaving him paralyzed from the waist down.

Is lethal injection more humane than other methods of execution?

What are the characteristics of the ideal mode of execution? What currently available method seems best?

Worse yet, Willie's well-publicized actions after his capture suggested that he had no remorse for what he had done. He had a Grim Reaper tattooed across his chest. At the trial for the kidnapping and rape charges for the Alabama incident, Willie blew kisses to the woman he had raped and made a throat-slashing gesture to the man he had tied to a tree and shot. He told a newspaper reporter, "Hey man, them people's dead. You ain't gonna bring them back by talking about it."[2]

When Prejean first met Willie on Louisiana's death row, she expected to meet "a wild-eyed, crazed, paranoid type," but she was surprised to find Willie a "polite, soft-spoken, obviously intelligent young man."[3] Nevertheless, she had to come to terms with his horrible crimes while she acted as his spiritual advisor. On numerous occasions she confronted him with what he had done, and he continued to claim that his accomplice was responsible for the crimes.

> **Should a convicted criminal's attitude play a role in determining his or her sentence?**
>
> **Which is more relevant — the attitude at the time of the offense or the attitude afterward and during the trial?**

Willie was defiant almost to the end, but his attitude changed somewhat after he was led to the electric chair. He addressed his murder victim's parents: "I hope you get some relief from my death. Killing people is wrong. That's why you've put me to death. It makes no difference whether it's citizens, countries, or governments. Killing is wrong."[4]

Although she realized that it would be a traumatic experience, Prejean decided to witness the execution:

> When the jolts hit him, the way he was strapped to the chair, his body didn't move much. He lifted somewhat in the chair and his chest pushed against the straps and his hands gripped the edge of the chair, but there wasn't much movement. Three times the current hit, and I couldn't see his face. I had prayed out loud, "God forgive us, forgive all who collaborate in this execution."[5]

The parents of Willie's victim, Faith Hathaway, also witnessed Willie's execution, expressing their satisfaction to the press afterward. Her stepfather poured himself a celebratory drink and asked a reporter, "Do you want to dance? First thing I'm gonna do is have a drink, then go home and rest."[6]

After the execution, Prejean wondered what had been accomplished. She asked a news reporter, "What have we accomplished by killing Robert Willie? Now two people are dead instead of one, and there will be another funeral and another mother will bury her child."[7] The Rev. Jesse Jackson echoed Prejean's sentiments:

> [T]he argument that capital punishment eases the grief of a victim's family is questionable, especially in a nation where there are only 25 executions for 25,000 murders each year. . . . [N]either the death penalty nor its alternatives can substitute for the tremendous loss of a loved one.[8]

When Prejean's book about her experiences, *Dead Man Walking* (1993), was made into a popular movie of the same name (1995), the news media ran coverage of the death penalty debate, and public interest was aroused. Public awareness of the issue is usually quite high, and each time an execution occurs, there is once again an increased interest in capital punishment's pros and cons.

Should a murder victim's family have a say in whether a convicted criminal is executed?

Does, or should, the family have the right to witness the execution?

Would it be in the public interest to televise executions?

Moral and Religious Issues

There is no clear-cut answer to whether moral or religious values support the death penalty. Some people argue that the Judeo-Christian Bible, which has greatly influenced American laws and morality, supports capital punishment. The Book of Exodus calls for punishment equal to the crime—"life for life, eye for eye, tooth for tooth." (Exodus 21: 23–24) However, many people question whether these standards are fair today: the

Sister Helen Prejean at a Louisiana prison. Prejean, who has served as a spiritual advisor to several death-row inmates, is one of the United States' best-known anti–death penalty activists.

same chapter declares that when one man's ox kills another man's servant, then the ox must be stoned to death and the ox's owner must pay the servant's master a sum of silver coins. (Exodus 21:32)

Today, many religious groups, including the Catholic Church, favor abolition of the death penalty. In 1995, Pope John Paul II wrote in his *Evangelium Vitae*:

> [T]he nature and extent of the punishment must be carefully evaluated and decided upon, and ought not go to the extreme of executing the offender except in cases of absolute necessity: in other words, when it would not be possible otherwise to defend society. Today however, as a result of steady improvements in the organization of the penal system, such cases are very rare, if not practically non-existent.[9]

Although much of the debate over the death penalty revolves around religious and moral questions that might never be resolved to most people's satisfaction, there are also a number of legal and sociological debates as to whether the United States should retain the death penalty. One of the primary reasons for administering the death penalty is to control crime, but many people question the death penalty's deterrent effect, and some people even assert that watching the government kill people makes citizens even more likely to commit murder.

Death penalty trials are complicated and always result in lengthy appeals in both the state and federal courts. Many people argue that the system should be streamlined so that criminals will be executed more swiftly. However, a great number of people think that our legal system does not provide enough safeguards; they point to the cases of innocent people who have been sentenced to death or even executed. In recent years, opponents of the death penalty have pointed to alternatives that they believe would also effectively deter crime, such as the possibility of a sentence of life in prison without parole. Each time an execution draws near, these topics are debated hotly.

> **Church and state are separated, in theory, by the U.S. Constitution and by tradition. How great an influence should religious leaders should have on legislation?**
>
> **What if those leaders represent the opinion of most Americans?**
>
> **What if they represent a small but powerful segment of the population?**

———•———•———•———

The death penalty is deeply rooted in history, but today, the United States is the only Western industrialized nation that continues to use capital punishment. Since the U.S. Supreme Court upheld the practice in *Gregg v. Georgia* (1976), people have been executed by a variety of methods; the most common method of execution today is lethal injection. Although a majority of Americans support the death penalty, it remains controversial. Abolitionists, those who oppose the death penalty, are very dedicated to their cause and very vocal, but capital punishment has many supporters, too. The death penalty is often a key issue in political races.

The Death Penalty Is an Effective Deterrent to Crime

When the U.S. Supreme Court ended a nationwide moratorium on executions with the ruling in *Gregg v. Georgia* (1976), the Court cited two major reasons for imposing the death penalty: retribution and deterrence. Death penalty opponents generally argue that retribution is morally unjustified, but they have taken the argument against deterrence a step further, claiming that its efficacy is not supported by the facts. Supporters of the death penalty reject this argument and believe that the death penalty *is* an effective deterrent against crime. In fact, many supporters believe that for each person who is executed, a number of innocent lives are saved.

Although the Supreme Court seemed to put the deterrence issue to rest in *Gregg* by stating that "there is no convincing empirical evidence either supporting or refuting" the deterrent effect of capital punishment,[1] abolitionists continue to argue that the death penalty is not a deterrent. Death penalty supporters therefore feel compelled to counter those arguments, arguing both that the deterrent effect of capital punishment is clear and that abolitionists' efforts to discount the deterrent effect miss the point. Professor John McAdams of Marquette University argues the point elegantly:

> If we execute murderers and there is in fact no deterrent effect, we have killed a bunch of murderers. If we fail to execute murderers, and doing so would in fact have deterred other murders, we have allowed the killing of a bunch of innocent victims. I would much rather risk the former. This, to me, is not a tough call.[2]

What key assumption does Professor McAdams make in this argument?

Is his assumption valid?

Common sense and experience demonstrate capital punishment's effectiveness as a deterrent to crime.

Some of the strongest arguments for the death penalty's deterrent value are based upon common sense. Put simply, people are afraid of dying, and therefore the possibility of being sentenced to death for committing certain crimes discourages people from committing those crimes. The experience of the U.S. criminal justice system supports this straightforward logic. Almost everyone who is sentenced to death appeals his or her sentence: obviously, these people do not wish to die. The inevitability of appeals seems to contradict abolitionists' claims that a sentence of life in prison without parole is as effective a deterrent as a death sentence.

The plea bargaining process also provides evidence that criminals fear the death penalty. A plea bargain is an arrangement between a prosecutor and a criminal defendant (or his or her lawyers) under which the defendant agrees to plead guilty and the prosecutor agrees to recommend a specific sentence. For example, a person who faces up to ten years in prison for a particular crime might agree to plead guilty in exchange for a two-year sentence. Prosecutors might offer a plea bargain for various reasons: a fear that the defendant might not be found guilty; an effort to shield a young or traumatized witness from having to testify in court; or a desire to avoid the time and expense of a trial.

The availability of the death penalty makes the plea

FROM THE BENCH

From *Gregg v. Georgia*, 428 U.S. 153 (1976)

The death penalty is said to serve two principal social purposes: retribution and deterrence of capital crimes by prospective offenders.

In part, capital punishment is an expression of society's moral outrage at particularly offensive conduct. This function may be unappealing to many, but it is essential in an ordered society that asks its citizens to rely on legal processes rather than self-help to vindicate their wrongs. . . . Indeed, the decision that capital punishment may be the appropriate sanction in extreme cases is an expression of the community's belief that certain crimes are themselves so grievous an affront to humanity that the only adequate response may be the penalty of death.

Statistical attempts to evaluate the worth of the death penalty as a deterrent to crimes by potential offenders have occasioned a great deal of debate. The results simply have been inconclusive. As one opponent of capital punishment has said:

> "[A]fter all possible inquiry, including the probing of all possible methods of inquiry, we do not know, and for systematic and easily visible reasons cannot know, what the truth about this 'deterrent' effect may be. . . .
>
> "The inescapable flaw is . . . that social conditions in any state are not constant through time, and that social conditions are not the same in any two states. If an effect were observed (and the observed effects, one way or another, are not large) then one could not at all tell whether any of this effect is attributable to the presence or absence of capital punishment. A 'scientific' — that is to say, a soundly based — conclusion is simply impossible, and no methodological path out of

bargaining process especially effective in murder trials. When one person is charged with killing another, the prosecutor generally has broad discretion to charge the defendant with any of a number of crimes, with names like first-degree murder, manslaughter, etc. Only certain categories of homicides (so-called "capital murder" offenses) are punishable by the death penalty, however. By agreeing not to charge the defendant with capital murder, a prosecutor can often persuade the

this tangle suggests itself." C. Black, *Capital Punishment: The Inevitability of Caprice and Mistake* 25–26 (1974).

Although some of the studies suggest that the death penalty may not function as a significantly greater deterrent than lesser penalties, there is no convincing empirical evidence either supporting or refuting this view. We may nevertheless assume safely that there are murderers, such as those who act in passion, for whom the threat of death has little or no deterrent effect. But for many others, the death penalty undoubtedly is a significant deterrent. There are carefully contemplated murders, such as murder for hire, where the possible penalty of death may well enter into the cold calculus that precedes the decision to act. And there are some categories of murder, such as murder by a life prisoner, where other sanctions may not be adequate.

The value of capital punishment as a deterrent of crime is a complex factual issue the resolution of which properly rests with the legislatures, which can evaluate the results of statistical studies in terms of their own local conditions and with a flexibility of approach that is not available to the courts. . . . [Many states' capital punishment] statutes reflect just such a responsible effort to define those crimes and those criminals for which capital punishment is most probably an effective deterrent.

In sum, we cannot say that the judgment of the Georgia Legislature that capital punishment may be necessary in some cases is clearly wrong. Considerations of federalism, as well as respect for the ability of a legislature to evaluate, in terms of its particular State, the moral consensus concerning the death penalty and its social utility as a sanction, require us to conclude, in the absence of more convincing evidence, that the infliction of death as a punishment for murder is not without justification and thus is not unconstitutionally severe.

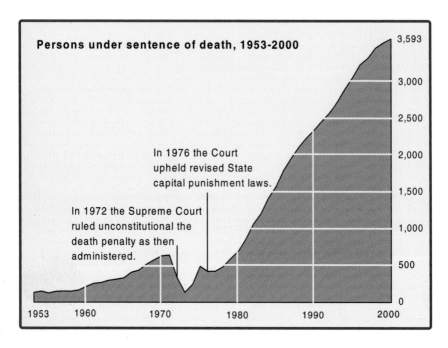

Persons under sentence of death, 1953-2000

3,593

3,000

2,500

2,000

1,500

In 1976 the Court
upheld revised State
capital punishment laws.

In 1972 the Supreme Court
ruled unconstitutional the
death penalty as then
administered.

1,000

500

0

1953   1960   1970   1980   1990   2000

defendant to plead guilty to a lesser charge. The fact that this
strategy works shows that criminal defendants fear the death
penalty, and this logic can be extended to suggest that because
criminals fear the death penalty, the availability of the death
penalty deters crime.

**Is plea bargaining fair, or
does it pressure innocent
people to plead guilty
in order to avoid the
death penalty?**

**Or does it cheat the
public out of retribution?**

Capital punishment is needed to curb crime rates.

Although the United States is a world
leader in wealth, technology, education, and industry, it nonetheless has
much higher crime rates than other
Western democracies. Although
politicians have for decades tried to improve the ability of law
enforcement agencies to prevent crime, the rates for many crimes
have continued to rise throughout the nation. According to crime
statistics published by the Federal Bureau of Investigation (FBI),

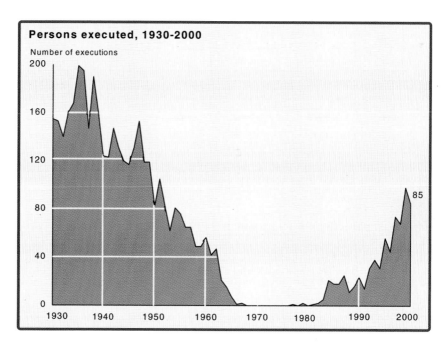

Persons executed, 1930-2000

the national murder rate increased 6.7 percent during the year 2001—even though the report excluded the terrorist acts of September 11 from the yearly total.

Sociologists blame many factors for the nation's high rate of violent crime. Problems such as drug abuse, gang membership, poverty, and the proliferation of illegal handguns are not easily solved. Law enforcement officials constantly struggle for increased resources, but even as crime rates continue to escalate, many police forces cannot keep pace. Supporters of the death penalty argue that because it is not feasible to end poverty or drug abuse through social programs, or to remove illegal handguns from the streets, the death penalty is needed to help law enforcement keep pace with crime. Supporters say that enforcing the death penalty on a regular basis will result in a statistical decrease in murders.

Is it appropriate to use a convicted criminal's efforts to avoid the death penalty as evidence that the death penalty deters crime?

A landmark 1975 study by economist Isaac Ehrlich attempted to quantify what death penalty supporters had been saying for years—that life lost to execution would save other lives by deterring murders. His study examined murder rates and execution rates nationally during the period from 1933 through 1967. Ehrlich acknowledged that "an apparent negative effect of execution on the murder rate" might be due to the obvious fact that the death penalty prevents people from killing again. However, based on his analysis, he concluded that "punishment in general, and execution in particular exert a unique deterrent effect on potential murderers." His analysis indicated that "an additional execution per year . . . may have resulted, on average, in 7 or 8 fewer murders." [3]

> **Why does the United States have such high crime rates?**
>
> **What factors might make it difficult to determine the answer?**

Criminals avoid committing crimes that carry the death penalty.

Many death penalty supporters believe that criminals know which crimes are punishable by death, and that criminals avoid these crimes. States specify "capital offenses" in their death penalty statutes in order to comply with the U.S. Supreme Court's decision in *Furman v. Georgia* (1972). The central holding was that death penalty statutes—as they stood in 1972—violated the Eighth Amendment's ban on "cruel and unusual punishment" because they did not set standards for the types of crimes for which the death penalty was given:

> [W]e deal with a system of law and of justice that leaves to the uncontrolled discretion of judges or juries the determination whether defendants committing these crimes should die or be imprisoned. Under these laws no standards govern the selection of the penalty. People live or die, dependent on the whim of one man or of 12.[4]

As a result of the decision in *Furman*, states rewrote their death penalty statutes, enumerating capital offenses. A common example is "felony murder," in which a murder is committed during the commission of another felony, such as armed robbery, rape, or kidnapping. Other capital offenses include murdering someone for money, hiring someone to murder another person, and murdering a police officer.

> Are some forms of murder worse, or more excusable, than others? If so, then how should the criminal justice system handle these variations?

Anecdotal evidence clearly indicates that the death penalty deters at least *some* crime: numerous criminals have told law enforcement officers that they specifically avoided committing capital offenses, as opposed to lesser crimes that do not carry the death penalty. For example, one study catalogued incidents from the 1950s through the 1970s in which criminals told law enforcement officials that they had "used a fake gun, pretended to be carrying a weapon, or refrained from killing a robbery victim to avoid the death penalty."[5] In the 1970s, the Los Angeles Police Department interviewed nearly a hundred criminals who had not carried weapons while committing crimes, and half of the criminals said fear of the death penalty was a reason for not carrying a weapon.

> If a murder occurs in the course of a robbery, should the murderer be held responsible for the death, even if he or she planned to commit only robbery?
>
> Are there important differences between the two crimes, or should this be considered strictly as a murder?

U.S. Senator Arlen Specter reported that, while a prosecutor in Philadelphia, "I saw many cases where professional burglars and robbers refused to carry weapons for fear that a killing would occur and they would be charged with murder in the first degree, carrying the death penalty."[6] The Senator gave as a specific example the story of three men who robbed a pharmacist: Two said that they would not participate if the third carried a gun. Although the third man pretended to put the gun away, he secretly brought it with him and ended up killing the pharmacist. The first two were spared the death penalty because they did not know that the third man carried the gun.

Capital punishment ensures that murderers will not kill again.

Supporters of the death penalty reject an argument frequently made by abolitionists—that the sentence of life in prison without possibility of parole is just as effective in deterring murders as the death penalty is. In particular, say death penalty supporters, the death penalty is needed to deter people who have already been convicted of murder from killing again because a sentence of life in prison without parole cannot achieve this objective.

The main flaw in substituting sentences of life in prison without parole for the death penalty, supporters say, is that such a sentence does not carry the finality of the death penalty. Although a person might be sentenced to life in prison without parole, there is no guarantee that the person will remain in prison forever. One possibility is that the state legislature might change the sentencing laws to allow people under such a sentence to qualify for parole, for example, through good behavior. Another possibility is that a person could use his or her time in prison to bring endless legal challenges to his or her conviction, perhaps ultimately overturning it on a technicality of law, such as a mistake in the search warrant.

> **How might the government "apologize" for a capital sentence handed down in error?**
>
> **Do you see a problem in enforcing a penalty, such as the death penalty, that cannot be reversed — or is this a risk inherent to the system?**

Of course, there is also the very real possibility that a person who is part of the general prison population and not kept on the more secure "death row" could eventually escape from prison.

By allowing the convicted criminal the possibility of one day regaining his or her freedom through legal or illegal means, the sentence of life in prison without parole does not deter crime as effectively as the death penalty. Death penalty supporters argue that a person sentenced to life in prison without parole—in the absence of a death penalty—might kill another prisoner or a prison guard. From a practical standpoint, the inmate already facing the maximum penalty allowed by law has no legal disincentive to kill again. With nothing to risk, and the only means to freedom being escape, logic says that a prisoner facing life in prison without parole would be likely to kill in order to escape.

Are prison guards safe around prisoners who have "nothing to lose"?

Are such prisoners more dangerous than other prisoners?

—————●———————●———————●—————

Many people believe that the death penalty deters crime and is therefore needed to curb soaring crime rates. Some arguments for deterrence are based upon common sense: criminals, once caught, make efforts to avoid the death penalty; criminals tell police that they avoid crimes punishable by death; and people who are executed obviously cannot kill other victims. Supporters of the death penalty frequently cite research indicating that each execution has the potential to prevent seven or eight murders.

The Death Penalty Is Not an Effective Deterrent to Crime

The theory that the death penalty deters crime is supported by anecdotes, such as those of criminals who refused to carry weapons because they feared the death penalty, and some studies, such as those conducted by Isaac Ehrlich, which assert that each execution deters approximately eight homicides. Nevertheless, many opponents of the death penalty steadfastly maintain that the death penalty does *not* deter crime. In fact, many abolitionists believe that the death penalty actually *encourages* crime.

Prior to Ehrlich's studies, economists and social scientists had attempted to discover a link between death penalty statutes and homicide rates. However, prior to Ehrlich's studies, no study had shown that capital punishment deters crime. Because Ehrlich's study relied upon complex mathematical equations, and because some of his methods are subject to debate, many abolitionists continue to rely upon earlier studies to support their claim that the death penalty does not have a deterrent effect. In fact, some studies have even suggested that murder rates actually *increase* after an execution. "

Statistics show that the death penalty does not deter crime.

The studies most frequently cited by abolitionists were conducted by criminologist Thorsten Sellin beginning in the 1950s. Sellin made two major types of comparisons. First, Sellin compared the homicide rates in sets of neighboring states, some of which had capital punishment and some of which did not. He compared the following states: Indiana and Ohio,

> Are you familiar with any of the states that Sellin studied?
>
> Is it fair to compare these sets of states?

which had a death penalty statute, to Michigan, which did not; Iowa (death penalty) to Minnesota and Wisconsin (no death penalty); South Dakota and Nebraska (death penalty) to North Dakota (no death penalty); New Hampshire and Vermont (death penalty) to Maine (no death penalty); and Massachusetts and Connecticut (death penalty) to Rhode Island (no death penalty).[1]

> What does it mean that Sellin's studies did not include the states with the most executions, such as Texas, Virginia, and Florida?

Second, in 1967 Sellin published a study examining changes in homicide rates in states that had either adopted a capital punishment statute or had eliminated the death penalty: Arizona, Colorado, Delaware, Iowa, Kansas, Maine, Missouri, Oregon, South Dakota, Tennessee, and Washington. The study found that neither instituting nor discontinuing the death penalty had any significant effect on the rate of homicide.[2]

In the years following Isaac Ehrlich's studies, a number of economists and social scientists attempted to support or disprove Ehrlich's assertion that each execution prevented eight murders. In his dissenting opinion to *Gregg v. Georgia* (1976), Justice Thurgood Marshall summarized the major criticisms of Ehrlich's conclusion that each execution prevented an average of eight homicides.

Marshall first pointed out that Ehrlich's study looked at the nation as a whole, rather than examining statistics on a state-by-state basis:

> It has been suggested, for example, that the study is defective because it compares execution and homicide rates on a nationwide, rather than a state-by-state, basis. The aggregation of data from all States—including those that have abolished the death penalty—obscures the relationship between murder and execution rates. Under Ehrlich's methodology, a decrease in the execution risk in one State combined with an increase in the murder rate in another State would, all other things being equal, suggest a deterrent effect that quite obviously would not exist. Indeed, a deterrent effect would be suggested if, once again all other things being equal, one State abolished the death penalty and experienced no change in the murder rate, while another State experienced an increase in the murder rate.[3]

In other words, Ehrlich failed to examine whether nationwide decreases in homicide rates were due to decreases in states that had the death penalty or in states that did not have the death penalty.

Does it seem that, regardless of statistics, the death penalty must prevent at least some murders?

Additionally, Marshall criticized Ehrlich's analysis because the results were not consistent during the entire

Justice Thurgood Marshall continued his crusade for civil rights after being appointed to the Supreme Court. Throughout his tenure on the Court, he remained a staunch opponent of the death penalty, which he maintained was "cruel and unusual punishment."

time period of the study, 1933 to 1969:

> The most compelling criticism of the Ehrlich study is that its conclusions are extremely sensitive to the choice of the time period included in the regression analysis. Analysis of Ehrlich's data reveals that all empirical support for the deterrent effect of capital punishment disappears when the five most recent years are removed from his time series—that is to say, whether a decrease in the execution risk corresponds to an increase or a decrease in the murder rate depends on the ending point of the sample period. This finding has cast severe doubts on the reliability of Ehrlich's tentative conclusions. Indeed, a recent regression study, based on Ehrlich's theoretical model but using cross-section state data for the years 1950 and 1960, found no support for the conclusion that executions act as a deterrent.

Essentially, Marshall accused Ehrlich of manipulating the data: Ehrlich's conclusions might have been valid for the years that he selected for his study. However, had Ehrlich chosen different years for the study, he would not have been able to establish that the death penalty deters homicides. Thus, Marshall concluded, "The Ehrlich study, in short, is of little, if any, assistance in assessing the deterrent impact of the death penalty."

Should a murderer be punished differently based on whether he or she was considering the consequences?

Murderers do not think about the consequences of their actions.

In addition to discounting statistical evidence supporting the death penalty, abolitionists offer philosophical and psychological explanations as to why the death penalty does not deter crime. In his book condemning the death penalty, *Legal Lynching*, Rev. Jesse Jackson offers the following theory:

Deterrence depends on would-be murderers identifying with the executed killer. The problem with that logic is that countless psychological studies show that we identify with those whom we admire or envy. Condemned prisoners who arrive at the electric chair are a wretched lot. Since they are generally loners who are uneducated and have committed brutal and cowardly crimes, it is highly unlikely that calculating killers would identify with them. The contrast they see between themselves and the condemned may actually lead prospective killers to determine that the death penalty is reserved only for people unlike themselves.[4]

> **Could public advertising campaigns — like those that have raised awareness of the fines for not wearing a seatbelt — make more people aware of the death penalty?**
>
> **Would this work with criminals?**

Abolitionists suggest that the very nature of most capital crimes makes them difficult to deter. For example, many murders are committed in the heat of passion, and the murderer is not thinking of the consequences of his or her actions. Consider this first-hand account:

[My wife] came out and said, "Look, please do me this favor and give me a divorce." At that moment I felt cold hatred for her inside me. . . . My hate for her exploded then, and I . . . started pounding her in the face with my fist. She put her arms up and covered her face, so I ran and got my rifle. . . . I got so mad and felt so much hate for her that I just started shooting her again and again.[5]

Abolitionists argue that even murderers "who cold-bloodedly plan and carry out their crimes . . . think they are too clever to be caught. The death penalty cannot be a deterrent to them because they are convinced they will escape punishment of any kind."[6]

One of the most famous murder cases of the 20th century illustrates this principle. Nathan Leopold Jr. and Richard Loeb were extremely intelligent young men who came from wealthy families and who shared a morbid desire to commit the perfect crime. After months of planning, on May 21, 1924, the pair kidnapped a teenage boy who lived in their affluent Chicago neighborhood. They then killed him and hid his body in a park in a remote part of the city. They went on with their social and academic activities as usual while trying to collect a ransom from the boy's father, to whom they represented that the boy was still alive. They never once imagined that they would be caught, and they probably would not have been, had Leopold not accidentally left a rare, expensive pair of eyeglasses at the crime scene. Killers who do not believe that they will be caught almost certainly do not consider possible punishments.

Should the death penalty be repealed because some murderers are not deterred by it?

Other murderers might be so out of touch with reality that they do not consider the consequences of their crimes. Gary Cone, a Vietnam veteran who was sentenced to death for a double homicide, explained that his experiences in Vietnam had caused him great distress that led to drug abuse and developing post-traumatic stress disorder (PTSD): "My visions in sleep were clouded by the sight of a buddy's head being blown off, and dying women and children I had seen left in the fields. The Vietcong would often torture and cut the children in half."[7]

In what other situations might witnessing violence lead to more violence?

After returning from Vietnam, Cone—like many Vietnam veterans—met with rejection everywhere, especially when he

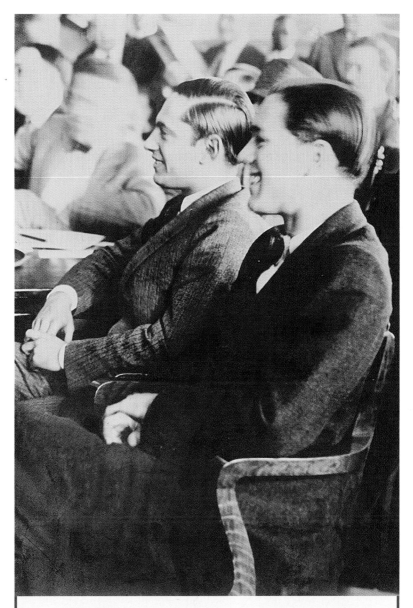

Nathan Leopold, Jr. and Richard Loeb, pictured laughing during their murder trial in 1924, killed a young boy for thrills. Many argue that the death penalty does not discourage cold-blooded killers.

looked for a job. Although he did not have a criminal history, he turned to a life of crime. Despite serving a short prison term, his criminal life continued to spiral out of control. According to court records:

> [Cone] robbed a Memphis jewelry store of approximately $112,000 in merchandise on a Saturday in August 1980. Shortly after the 12:45 p.m. robbery, a police officer in an unmarked vehicle spotted respondent driving at a normal speed and began to follow him. After a few blocks, respondent accelerated, prompting a high-speed chase through midtown Memphis and into a residential neighborhood where respondent abandoned his vehicle. Attempting to flee, respondent shot an officer who tried to apprehend him, shot a citizen who confronted him, and, at gunpoint, demanded that another hand over his car keys. As a police helicopter hovered overhead, respondent tried to shoot the fleeing car owner, but was frustrated because his gun was out of ammunition.
>
> Throughout the afternoon and into the next morning, respondent managed to elude detection as police combed the surrounding area. In the meantime, officers inventorying his car found an array of illegal and prescription drugs, the stolen merchandise, and more than $2,400 in cash. Respondent reappeared early Sunday morning when he drew a gun on an elderly resident who refused to let him in to use her telephone. Later that afternoon, respondent broke into the home of Shipley and Cleopatra Todd, aged 93 and 79 years old, and killed them by repeatedly beating them about the head with a blunt instrument. He moved their bodies so that they would not be visible from the front and rear doors and ransacked the first floor of their home. After shaving his beard, respondent traveled to Florida. He was arrested there for robbing a drugstore in Pompano Beach. He admitted killing the Todds and shooting the police officer.[8]

Cone claims the shootout with the police caused him to have a "flashback": "[T]he shooting . . . and the tear gas brought my mind swiftly back to the jungles of Vietnam. . . . I actually thought I was back in the war." While "on the lam," he killed the elderly Todds: "[T]wo people were dead. I don't remember killing them, but I know I must have. I remember thinking I was in the jungle of Vietnam, with the Cong chasing me, trying to kill me before I was arrested."[9]

The Supreme Court recently acknowledged that many murderers are not deterred by the threat of the death penalty: it held in *Atkins v. Virginia* (2002) that the Eighth Amendment's ban on cruel and unusual punishment prevented states from executing mentally retarded people. The Court ruled that the "diminished ability to understand and process information" of people with mental retardion: ". . . make[s] it less likely that they can process the information of the possibility of execution as a penalty and, as a result, control their conduct based upon that information."[10]

The death penalty can actually increase crime rates.

Perhaps the strongest argument against the deterrent effect of capital punishment can be found in a number of studies that indicate that the homicide rate actually *increases* after an execution. Studies conducted in London, Philadelphia, Oklahoma, and California show a significant increase in homicides in the city or state shortly after an execution took place. In 1980 William Bowers and Glenn Pierce examined homicide rates during the period from 1907 to 1963 in New York, which at the time was the state that executed the most people. Homicide rates generally rose in a month that followed an execution. Bowers and Pierce explained this surprising result through the "brutalization" theory—that when the state takes a person's life by execution, it devalues human life in the eyes of its citizens, making them more likely to commit murder.[11]

Michael Kroenenwetter offers alternative theories as to why the threat of the death penalty might actually encourage murder:

> The threat of capital punishment raises the stakes of getting caught. Anyone already subject to the death penalty has little to lose by killing again and again. Their potential sentence cannot be made any worse than it already is. This means that criminals who already face death for previous crimes are more likely to kill to avoid capture.[12]

Additionally, once captured, a prisoner facing the death penalty has nothing to lose by killing guards or fellow prisoners.

Anecdotal evidence suggests that some people actually look at the death penalty as a means of committing suicide. For example, before his 1992 execution Lloyd Wayne Hampton gave the following reason for having murdered a 69-year-old man:

> I had given up trying to make it. What was I going to do? . . . I either had to put myself in a position of being killed by someone else or committing suicide. At that point, I had strong beliefs about not killing myself. . . . So I put myself in a position to have the state kill me.[13]

Given the delays associated with executions, does "suicide by execution" seem improbable?

Measuring the deterrent effect of capital punishment is difficult and requires making broad assumptions and using complicated calculations. To some abolitionists like Rev. Jesse Jackson, studies to date simply do not provide support for the death penalty:

> If we as a society continue to impose the ultimate sanction on those who take the lives of others based on the belief that this will save lives, we need to have absolute, undeniable,

incontrovertible proof that deterrence really works. The moral responsibility in deciding the fate of another human being is simply too great for anything less. My investigation into decades of deterrence research reveals that there is no such evidence. Not even close.[14]

Abolitionists dispute the deterrent effect of the death penalty, accusing supporters of manipulating statistics: when similar states are compared, crime rates are not lower in states with the death penalty. Abolitionists attribute the lack of deterrence to the reality that criminals either do not think about the consequences of their actions or believe that they will never be caught.

Streamlining Capital Punishment Would Make It More Effective

Although most death penalty supporters believe that the death penalty *does* have a powerful deterrent effect, one answer to abolitionists' arguments against deterrence is that the death penalty would be much more effective if convicted criminals were executed much more swiftly. When a convicted criminal is sentenced to death, it is not only the end of a lengthy trial requiring great effort on the parts of the prosecutors and the court system, but also the beginning, in most cases, of a lengthy process of appealing the sentence to higher courts, perhaps all the way to the U.S. Supreme Court. The appeals process can take many years, and in many states, appeals courts are required to hear appeals of all death sentences, regardless of the merits of the case.

An 8'-by-10' "deathwatch" cell, where condemned criminals spend the final days of their lives. Many sentenced to death might not see these cells for decades—or ever—because of the lengthy appeals process.

Capital trials are too lengthy and impose too great a cost on the court system.

A capital trial is very different from other criminal trials, even other murder trials. Because of procedural safeguards imposed by the U.S. Supreme Court, state courts, and state statutes, a capital trial lasts longer and requires more money than other criminal trials. Although people commonly

Should the states help county courts to pay for capital trials?

attribute the cost of capital punishment to the post-trial appeals process, recent studies confirm that "the bulk of death penalty costs occur at the *trial* level."[1] As a result, many smaller counties are experiencing financial crises caused by death penalty trials, and more and more district attorneys are hesitating to seek the death penalty.

Many of the costs are procedural. In other criminal trials, a judge determines the sentence. However, capital trials include a separate sentencing phase in front of a jury, which must make the decision whether or not to impose the death penalty. Other costs are due to special efforts taken to provide the jury with as much information as possible upon which to base its determination of guilt or innocence and its decision whether or not to impose the death penalty. For example, in capital cases, two public defenders are assigned to defendants who cannot afford to hire their own lawyers, as opposed to other criminal cases, in which the defendant is entitled to only one court-appointed lawyer. Additionally, investigators and expert witnesses—who testify about crime scene evidence or the defendant's intelligence or sanity, for example—are common in capital cases, and the cost of hiring them is typically borne by the court system.

As might be expected, defense lawyers in capital cases typically take extra efforts to prevent their clients from being sentenced to death. As trials grow longer, they impose more costs on the court system. The jury selection process in capital trials is a painstaking process in which potential jurors are asked about their opinions on capital punishment, and many more potential jurors are typically refused than in other criminal proceedings. Additionally, defense lawyers typically make many motions to exclude evidence, each of which must be ruled upon by the judge. The result of the special procedures used in capital trials is that imposing the death penalty on a defendant can be extremely expensive. Abolitionist Richard Dieter notes:

In Texas, a death penalty case costs taxpayers an average of $2.3 million, about three times the cost of imprisoning someone in a single cell at the highest security level for 40 years. In Florida, each execution is costing the state $3.2 million.[2]

Although Dieter and other critics cite high costs as a reason to abolish the death penalty, supporters of the death penalty believe that the solution is to streamline the legal process by eliminating some of the procedural safeguards. However, pro–death penalty federal judge Alex Kozinski believes that because overturning U.S. Supreme Court jurisprudence would be impractical, if not impossible, a more practical approach is needed: "[S]tate legislatures should draft narrow statutes that reserve the death penalty for only the most heinous criminals . . . mass murderers, hired killers, airplane bombers, for example."[3]

> **Do the high costs of execution support the argument that the death penalty should be abolished — or the argument that it is too difficult to execute criminals?**

Although such a solution would involve a compromise by death penalty supporters, Kozinski believes that it would allow "the people, through their elected representatives [to] reassert meaningful control over the process," rather than allowing the courts to decide "on an ad hoc, irrational basis" who lives and who dies. To many death penalty supporters, however, it is the courts, and not the public, who should be willing to compromise.

> **Is limiting the number of crimes that merit the death penalty a reasonable solution?**
>
> **Would this dampen its deterrent effect?**

The jury is denied important information in the sentencing hearing.

In order to protect the rights of criminal defendants, criminal procedure places limits on information that a jury is allowed to hear. Although victims' rights advocates won a major victory in

Payne v. Tennessee (1991), some say that more reforms are needed. An example of a protection that some death penalty supporters believe is excessive is the rule established by *Dawson v. Delaware* (1992). In that case, the U.S. Supreme Court overturned the death sentence of David Dawson, who had been convicted of brutally murdering a woman and stealing her car after he had escaped from prison. Although the trial judge did not allow the prosecutors to introduce evidence that Dawson had Nazi symbols tattooed all over his body, the judge did allow the prosecutor to introduce evidence that Dawson belonged to the Aryan Brotherhood, "a white racist prison gang." The Court held that the evidence violated Dawson's "First Amendment . . . right to join groups and associate with others holding similar beliefs," reasoning:

> **Is it fair, for example, to allow a defendant to introduce evidence that he belonged to the Cub Scouts as a child if prosecutors cannot introduce evidence that he now belongs to a racist gang?**

> Even if the Delaware group to which Dawson allegedly belongs is racist, those beliefs, so far as we can determine, had no relevance to the sentencing proceeding in this case. For example, the Aryan Brotherhood evidence was not tied in any way to the murder of Dawson's victim.[3]

In a dissent, Justice Clarence Thomas warned that the Court's decision resulted in a "double standard" that prevented the jury from developing a true sense of the defendant's character:

> To prove his good character . . . Dawson introduced evidence that he had acted kindly toward his family, and that he had earned good time credits while in prison. . . . Dawson also introduced evidence of his membership and participation in various respectable organizations, including the Green Tree Program (described only as a "drug and alcohol program"),

Alcoholics Anonymous . . . and certain therapy and counseling groups. . . .

The Court's opinion suggests that the Constitution now imposes a double standard for determining relevance: a standard easy for defendants to satisfy, but difficult for prosecutors. [A] capital defendant has a right to introduce all relevant mitigating evidence. Capital defendants, as a result, regularly introduce character evidence that allows juries to consider their abstract beliefs and associational rights . . . for example, membership in a church . . . religious rebirth . . . conversion to Christianity . . . [and] former membership in the Cub Scouts[.] I see no way to hold that this evidence has relevance, but that Dawson's gang membership does not.

A double standard for determining relevance may distort the picture presented to the jury. In this case, Dawson himself chose to introduce evidence of certain good character traits. Unless the State had responded with evidence of other, bad traits, the jury could not possibly have made a fair and balanced determination. Membership in Alcoholics Anonymous might suggest a good character, but membership in the Aryan Brotherhood just as surely suggests a bad one. The jury could not have assessed Dawson's overall character without both.[4]

The appeals process is too lengthy and costly.

The appeals process for a criminal sentenced to death can last decades, in part because a condemned criminal can appeal his or her conviction to the state's appeals courts and supreme court, each of which might overturn the decision, order the lower court to reexamine an issue, or call

(continued on page 50)

Is it fair to families of murder victims to allow numerous appeals?

How many chances to appeal should a convicted criminal get?

THE LETTER OF THE LAW

From the Antiterrorism and Effective Death Penalty Act of 1996 (AEDPA)

§2254. State custody; remedies in Federal courts

(a) The Supreme Court . . . shall entertain an application for a writ of habeas corpus in behalf of a person in custody pursuant to the judgment of a State court only on the ground that he is in custody in violation of the Constitution or laws or treaties of the United States.

(b) (1) An application for a writ of habeas corpus on behalf of a person in custody pursuant to the judgment of a State court [generally] shall not be granted unless it appears that . . . the applicant has exhausted the remedies available in the courts of the State[.]

  (2) An application for a writ of habeas corpus may be denied on the merits, notwithstanding the failure of the applicant to exhaust the remedies available in the courts of the State. . . .

(d) An application for a writ of habeas corpus on behalf of a person in custody pursuant to the judgment of a State court [generally] shall not be granted with respect to any claim that was adjudicated on the merits in State court proceedings. . . .

(e) (1) In a proceeding instituted by an application for a writ of habeas corpus by a person in custody pursuant to the judgment of a State court, a determination of a factual issue made by a State court shall be presumed to be correct. The applicant shall have the burden of rebutting the presumption of correctness by clear and convincing evidence. . . .

(i) The ineffectiveness or incompetence of counsel during Federal or State collateral post-conviction proceedings shall not be a ground for relief. . . .

§2263. Filing of habeas corpus application; time requirements; tolling rules

(a) Any application . . . for habeas corpus relief . . . must be filed in the appropriate district court not later than 180 days after final State court affirmance of the conviction . . . [but this time may be extended by] an additional period not to exceed 30 days, if . . . a showing of good cause is made. . . .

§2264. Scope of Federal review; district court adjudications

(a) Whenever a State prisoner under capital sentence files a petition for habeas corpus relief to which this chapter applies, the district court shall only consider a claim or claims that have been raised and decided on the merits in the State courts, unless the failure to raise the claim properly is —

(1) the result of State action in violation of the Constitution or laws of the United States;

(2) the result of the Supreme Court's recognition of a new Federal right that is made retroactively applicable; or

(3) based on a factual predicate that could not have been discovered through the exercise of due diligence in time to present the claim for State or Federal post-conviction review....

§2266. Limitation periods for determining applications and motions

(a) The adjudication of any application...by a person under sentence of death, shall be given priority by the district court and by the court of appeals over all noncapital matters.

(b) (1) (A) A district court shall render a final determination and enter a final judgment on any application for a writ of habeas corpus brought under this chapter in a capital case not later than 180 days after the date on which the application is filed.

(B) A district court shall afford the parties at least 120 days in which to complete all actions, including the preparation of all pleadings and briefs, and if necessary, a hearing, prior to the submission of the case for decision.

(C) (i) A district court may delay for not more than one additional 30-day period beyond the period specified in subparagraph (A), the rendering of a determination of an application for a writ of habeas corpus if the court issues a written order making a finding, and stating the reasons for the finding, that the ends of justice that would be served by allowing the delay outweigh the best interests of the public and the applicant in a speedy disposition of the application....

(iii) No delay in disposition shall be permissible because of general congestion of the court's calendar....

(3) The time limitations under this section shall not be construed to entitle an applicant to a stay of execution, to which the applicant would otherwise not be entitled, for the purpose of litigating any application or appeal.

(4) (A) The failure of a court to meet or comply with a time limitation under this section shall not be a ground for granting relief from a judgment of conviction or sentence.

(continued from page 47)

for a whole new trial. Additionally, someone convicted in state court may appeal his or her conviction or death sentence to federal district courts, appeals courts, and the U.S. Supreme Court through a process known as *habeas corpus.* Although death penalty supporters won a major victory with the passage of the Antiterrorism and Effective Death Penalty Act of 1996, which limits the use of the habeas corpus process by condemned criminals, the appeals process can still go on—seemingly forever.

Gary Cone, the Vietnam veteran who was convicted in 1982 of killing an elderly couple two years earlier, had an appeal heard by the U.S. Supreme Court in 2002—twenty years after his death sentence. The appeal concerned an issue that Cone initially raised in 1984—that his trial lawyer had failed to provide him with effective representation because he had passed up the opportunity to offer a closing argument. Although a number of state and federal courts accepted the lawyer's explanation that it had been a strategic decision based upon the tone of the proceedings, a federal appeals court overruled the previous decisions. The state appealed the decision, and the U.S. Supreme Court reversed the lower court, upholding Cone's conviction and death sentence in *Bell v. Cone* (2002).

The Court did not decide whether or not Cone's lawyer had provided him with ineffective representation. Rather, because the Tennessee Court of Appeals had already decided this issue, the Supreme Court did not have to decide the issue based on the facts. Because the Antiterrorism and Effective Death Penalty Act of 1996 limits federal habeas corpus proceedings, the only issue before the Supreme Court was whether "the Tennessee Court of Appeals [had] applied [the law] to the facts of his case in an objectively unreasonable manner."[5] Although

Does AEDPA seem fair?

Aren't appeals courts supposed to review other courts' decisions?

Time under sentence of death and execution, by race, 1977-2000

Year of execution	Number executed			Average elapse time from sentence to execution for:		
	All races*	White	Black	All races*	White	Black
Total	683	423	248	121 mo	116 mo	128 mo
1977-83	11	9	2	51 mo	49 mo	58 mo
1984	21	13	8	74	76	71
1985	18	11	7	71	65	80
1986	18	11	7	87	78	102
1987	25	13	12	86	78	96
1888	11	6	5	80	72	89
1989	16	8	8	95	78	112
1990	23	16	7	95	97	91
1991	14	7	7	116	124	107
1992	31	19	11	114	104	135
1993	38	23	14	113	112	121
1994	31	20	11	122	117	132
1995	56	33	22	134	128	144
1996	45	31	14	125	112	153
1997	74	45	27	133	126	147
1998	68	48	18	130	128	132
1999	98	61	33	143	143	141
2000	85	49	35	137	134	142

Note: Average time was calculated from the most recent sentencing date.
*Includes American Indians and Asians.

the Supreme Court's decision seemingly put an end to the ordeal of the families of Cone's victims, many death penalty supporters argue that further reforms are needed, because 20 years is too long for victims' families to wait.

Many argue that it is too difficult to execute criminals for their crimes. Capital trials are long and expensive and offer too many protections to accused criminals. The appeals process can last for decades; although a recent federal law should curb the appeals process somewhat, many would like to see further reforms.

It Is Already Too Easy to Convict and Execute People

Despite claims from death penalty supporters, victims' rights groups, and prosecutors that enforcing the death penalty is too difficult and costly, many abolitionists steadfastly believe that the opposite is true: that it is too easy to convict someone and sentence him or her to death. In addition to criticizing specific elements of the capital trial and sentencing procedures, abolitionists also point to examples of cases in which people have been wrongfully sentenced to death or even executed.

Victims' families play too great a role in imposing capital punishment.

In the early 1980s, in response to court decisions expanding the rights of the accused, crime victims and their families—and the families of murder victims—began to organize the victims' rights movement. Many states have passed victims' rights laws, which—for example—require victims and their families to be notified of criminal proceedings, entitle them to monetary compensation, and guarantee their right to testify at trials and sentencing hearings.

Until 1991, however, crime victims' families did not have the right to offer testimony at sentencing hearings in capital trials. The Supreme Court had held, in cases such as *Booth v. Maryland* (1987), that "victim impact statements," which describe how a crime has affected murder victims' families, were not admissible. John Booth had murdered an elderly Baltimore couple, and in the victim impact statement prepared by the Division of Parole and Probation:

> **Do you think that crime victims and their families deserve the same rights as the accused, or do the accused need rights that protect them from wrongful convictions?**
>
> **Do victims' families need special rights?**

> The son, for example, said that he suffers from lack of sleep and depression, and is "fearful for the first time in his life." ... He said that in his opinion, his parents were "butchered like animals." . . . The daughter said she also suffers from lack of sleep, and that since the murders she has become withdrawn and distrustful. She stated that she can no longer watch violent movies or look at kitchen knives without being reminded of the murders.[1]

The Court overturned Booth's sentence, reasoning that although "[o]ne can understand the grief and anger of the family," the victim impact statement would "inflame the jury" and prevent it from basing its sentence on "relevant evidence."[2]

> **Isn't it natural for juries to be "inflamed" by brutal murders?**

Four years later, the Court reversed itself, holding in *Payne v. Tennessee* (1991) that victim impact statements are admissible. While even steadfast abolitionists acknowledge the validity of the anger of crime victims and their families—Sister Helen Prejean has been active in victim support groups—abolitionists do not believe that this anger serves as a justification for capital punishment. Abolitionists believe that the Supreme Court went too far in *Payne*. As Justice Stevens noted in his dissent, the decision tipped the balance against the defendant and greatly increased the probability of execution, based on

FROM THE BENCH

From *Payne v. Tennessee*, 501 U.S. 808 (1991)

[F]or the jury to assess meaningfully the defendant's moral culpability and blameworthiness, it should have before it at the sentencing phase evidence of the specific harm caused by the defendant. "[T]he State has a legitimate interest in counteracting the mitigating evidence which the defendant is entitled to put in, by reminding the sentencer that just as the murderer should be considered as an individual, so too the victim is an individual whose death represents a unique loss to society and in particular to his family." ... [T]urning the victim into a "faceless stranger at the penalty phase of a capital trial" ... may prevent the jury from having before it all the information necessary to determine the proper punishment for a first-degree murder.

The present case is an example of the potential for such unfairness. The capital sentencing jury heard testimony from Payne's girlfriend that they met at church; that he was affectionate, caring, and kind to her children; that he was not an abuser of drugs or alcohol; and that it was inconsistent with his character to have committed the murders. Payne's parents testified that he was a good son, and a clinical psychologist testified that Payne was an extremely polite prisoner and suffered from a low IQ. ... In contrast, the only evidence of the impact of Payne's offenses ... was Nicholas' grandmother's description ... that the child misses his mother and baby sister. ... [T]here is nothing unfair about allowing the jury to bear in mind that harm at the same time as it considers the mitigating evidence introduced by the defendant. The Supreme Court of Tennessee ... said: "It is an affront

factors other than the defendant's guilt:

> Today's majority has obviously been moved by an argument that has strong political appeal but no proper place in a reasoned judicial opinion. Because [the law] recognizes the defendant's right to introduce all mitigating evidence that may inform the jury about his character, the Court suggests that fairness requires that the State be allowed to respond with similar evidence about the victim. . . . This argument is a classic non sequitur: The victim is not on trial; her character, whether good or bad, cannot therefore constitute either an aggravating or a mitigating circumstance. . . .

to the civilized members of the human race to say that at sentencing in a capital case, a parade of witnesses may praise the background, character and good deeds of Defendant (as was done in this case), without limitation as to relevancy, but nothing may be said that bears upon the character of, or the harm imposed upon, the victims." . . .

. . . Under the aegis of the Eighth Amendment, we have given the broadest latitude to the defendant to introduce relevant mitigating evidence reflecting on his individual personality, and the defendant's attorney may argue that evidence to the jury. Petitioner's attorney in this case did just that. For the reasons discussed above, we now reject the view . . . that a State may not permit the prosecutor to similarly argue to the jury the human cost of the crime of which the defendant stands convicted. We reaffirm the view expressed by Justice Cardozo in *Snyder v. Massachusetts*, 291 U.S. 97, 122 (1934): "[J]ustice, though due to the accused, is due to the accuser also. The concept of fairness must not be strained till it is narrowed to a filament. We are to keep the balance true."

We thus hold that if the State chooses to permit the admission of victim impact evidence and prosecutorial argument on that subject, the Eighth Amendment erects no per se bar. A State may legitimately conclude that evidence about the victim and about the impact of the murder on the victim's family is relevant to the jury's decision as to whether or not the death penalty should be imposed. There is no reason to treat such evidence differently than other relevant evidence is treated.

The Constitution grants certain rights to the criminal defendant and imposes special limitations on the State designed to protect the individual from overreaching by the disproportionately powerful State.[3]

The jury selection process is unfair to defendants.

Jurors are chosen from a pool of potential jurors called the *venire facias* (or *venire*) in a process called *voir dire*. In criminal trials, prosecutors try to exclude jurors whom they feel are more likely to find the defendant not guilty; defense attorneys similarly try to exclude jurors thought more likely to convict. Many believe that people from minority groups are less likely to convict than whites; however, because it is illegal to exclude jurors solely because of their race, prosecutors often look for other rationales to exclude jurors. This requires often extensive questioning about whether a potential juror has been a crime victim, how he or she feels about crime, etc.

During the voir dire for capital trials, prosecutors engage in the process of "death qualification." The prosecution is able to exclude any juror who says that he or she would not be willing to impose the death penalty if selected as a juror; the U.S. Supreme Court upheld this practice in *Witherspoon v. Illinois* (1968). While holding that people cannot be excluded from a jury for simply expressing general misgivings about capital punishment, the Court held that potential jurors *can* be excluded for saying that they could not apply the death penalty to the defendant in that particular case. In *Witherspoon*, the counsel for the condemned prisoner had claimed:

Does excluding jurors who do not believe in the death penalty "stack the deck" against the defendant?

Does it matter? What can be done to correct this?

> [A jury that has been "death-qualified"], unlike one chosen at
> random from a cross-section of the community, must neces-
> sarily be biased in favor of conviction, for the kind of juror
> who would be unperturbed by the prospect of sending a man
> to his death . . . is the kind of juror who would too readily
> ignore the presumption of the defendant's innocence . . . and
> return a verdict of guilt.[4]

The Court rejected the argument:

> We simply cannot conclude . . . that the exclusion of jurors
> opposed to capital punishment results in an unrepresentative
> jury on the issue of guilt or substantially increases the risk
> of conviction.[5]

Critics of the death penalty dispute the Court's conclusion
in *Witherspoon* and strongly believe that excluding potential
jurors who would not impose the death penalty violates a
defendant's constitutional rights. Houston attorney Clay S.
Conrad blames death qualification for increasing the amount of
time that it takes to select capital juries and for removing a
larger percentage of women and minorities than of white
men: "That may explain why capital juries are approximately
43 percent more likely to sentence a killer to die if his victim is
white." The result of death qualification is that capital juries "are
not only biased towards death (instead of life imprisonment),
but conviction," and that of the thousands of inmates on death
row, "not a single one has received a trial before a jury representative of the community. . . . "[6]

Sentencing can be unfairly influenced by public pressure.

Although the Constitution guarantees the accused the right to
a fair trial and freedom from cruel and unusual punishment,
public pressure plays a role—too great a role, abolitionists say—

in determining whether a district attorney will seek the death penalty in any given case. Because district attorneys are either elected officials or political appointees, public satisfaction does play a role in whether they keep their jobs.

Should public opinion play a role in how criminal trials are prosecuted?

If a criminal trial is supposed to be "the people" against the defendant, shouldn't public opinion matter?

In the context of a criminal trial, what does "the people" mean?

Even though jury deliberations are supposed to remain secret, many times a jury feels public pressure to enforce the death penalty. Because of the widespread public perception that murderers frequently are released after serving very little time, members of the jury do not want to be blamed for returning a vicious killer to the streets. Because of public pressure, abolitionists argue, a sentence of death is often not the result of a fair trial.

Worse, because public pressure often depends on the race of the accused or the victim, the effect of uneven public pressure is uneven application of the death penalty. Unfortunately, incidents show that racism often plays a role in the decisions whether to convict and whether to sentence to death. In the summer of 1980, when a white teenage girl was raped and murdered inside a Conroe, Texas high school while a volleyball game was being played outside, the community demanded that the perpetrator be brought to justice and put great pressure on law enforcement officials—parents

How can the courts ensure a fair trial for an African-American person in a mostly white community in which many people hold racist views?

Is a truly fair trial always possible?

even threatened to keep their children home from school. When Clarence Brandley, an African-American man, was arrested and first brought to trial, he faced an all-white jury in a county that was only about five percent African-American. There was very little evidence against Brandley, but the jury voted eleven to one for conviction. William Srack, the juror who dissented, was called a "nigger-lover" by his fellow jurors and received threatening and harassing phone calls for months after the trial. At a second trial, an all-white jury convicted Brandley and sentenced him to death.

Innocent people can be sentenced to death.

Today Clarence Brandley is a free man: more than a decade after the crime, all charges were dropped. Despite strong evidence that someone else had committed the crime, Brandley had come within six days of execution. Abolitionists cite cases like Brandley's to support their argument that all of the legal safeguards that a defendant has on paper can break down in the real-life court room, resulting in innocent people being condemned to death.

The Brandley case began in August of 1980 with the rape and murder of 16-year-old Cheryl Fergeson, the manager of a visiting girls' volleyball team, at Conroe High School. Brandley was the supervisor of the janitorial staff, and he also happened to be the only African-American. When Brandley and another janitor found Fergeson's body, suspicion began to focus on Brandley almost immediately. According to the testimony of the other janitor, a police officer said to them, "One of you two is going to hang for this," and then said to Brandley, "Since you're the nigger, you're elected."[7] After the first trial, which ended in a hung jury because of the dissent of juror William Srack (whom Rev. Jesse Jackson observes "almost became a hung juror,"[8] quite literally), Brandley was convicted at the second trial.

The evidence at the second trial was conflicting. Circumstantial evidence pointed to Brandley: Other janitors testified to having seen Brandley headed toward the bathroom where Fergeson had last been seen. He had told the other janitors to meet him at another building but had not met them for 45 minutes. During the search for Fergeson, he had asked another janitor to search the loft in which Fergeson's body would later be found—not once, but three times, after the first two searches had failed to discover her body concealed under a piece of plywood. However, although this circumstantial evidence pointed to Brandley, there was no physical evidence linking him to the crime.

> **If a jury votes eleven to one to convict, should the defendant receive a new trial?**

Several red hairs—which could not have belonged to either Fergeson or Brandley—had been found on the body. The second jury convicted Brandley in 1981, but when Brandley attempted to appeal his conviction, some physical evidence, including the hairs and semen samples, had been destroyed or discarded.

With circumstantial evidence implicating him, and the physical evidence missing, Brandley's appeals were fruitless. His first break came in 1986, when a woman from a nearby town— who claimed to have heard nothing previously of the crime or the trials—came forward to say that her former common-law husband had told her in 1980 that he had killed a woman, but that she had not believed him until she heard about Fergeson's murder years later. This man, James Robinson, had been a janitor at Conroe High and had been fired not long before the murder. Another janitor, Gary Acreman, who had testified at Brandley's trial, recanted his trial testimony and told investigators a new story implicating Robinson; Acreman's nervous, contradictory stories made investigators suspect that Acreman also might have been involved.

Despite the new evidence, Brandley's appeals continued to be unsuccessful until March 1987, when he received a stay of execution only six days before he was scheduled to die. A trial judge, after reviewing the evidence in the case, recommended to the Court of Criminal Appeals in October 1987 that Brandley be given a new trial in another county, where racism and publicity would play less of a role. However, Brandley remained on death row for two more years. Finally, in December 1989, the court granted him a new trial, and in January 1990, Clarence Brandley was released on bail after spending nine years in prison. When the U.S. Supreme Court upheld the order of a new trial, the district attorney finally dropped the charges against Brandley in October 1990.

> **If circumstantial evidence was enough to convict Brandley, shouldn't it have been enough to earn him a new trial?**

Brandley's case is one of the best-publicized cases of an innocent person spending time on death row. But it is not the only case. A study by abolitionists Hugo Adam Bedau and Michael Radelet published in 1987 in *Stanford Law Review* uncovered 350 cases in which people were convicted of capital crimes although evidence later indicated that they were innocent.[9] For many, the margin of error might be small, but due to the irreversible nature of the death penalty, *any* margin of error is too great.

> **Do you agree that even one wrongful execution is too many?**
>
> **What about innocent lives that might be saved by retaining the death penalty?**

———————•—————————•—————————•———————

Abolitionists argue for greater safeguards. Juries are chosen from among death penalty supporters who are more likely to convict, and they listen to inflammatory testimony from the victims' families. Innocent people have been sentenced to death.

Capital Punishment Is a Just Process

Claims of racial discrimination always grab headlines, but many feel that "playing the race card" can divert people's attention from real issues. For example, in the O.J. Simpson murder trial, his lawyers made great efforts to label the Los Angeles Police Department as racist. The "not guilty" verdict was widely criticized: perhaps some, or even many, police officers were racist—but did that racism have any bearing on the determination of whether Simpson killed Nicole Brown Simpson and Ronald Goldman?

People accused Simpson's defense lawyers of "playing the race card"—

> Do juries play a role in reforming police departments by refusing to convict people arrested by those police departments?
>
> Do police play a fair role in deciding who is accused of a crime?

Many oppose the death penalty because they believe that the criminal justice system in the United States applies the death penalty in a racially discriminatory manner. Allegations of racism played a major role in the murder trial of former football star O.J. Simpson.

diverting attention from substantive issues by charging that racism tainted the proceedings. The "race card" is also frequently played in capital murder trials and appeals. Defense attorneys and abolitionists frequently claim that one of the major problems with capital punishment is that it is applied unfairly to minorities, the poor, and the undereducated. By contrast, death penalty supporters believe that legal safeguards currently in place are sufficient to deter discrimination in sentencing, and that it is unfair to draw broad generalities based on sentences that are specific to each case.

The death penalty is not applied in a discriminatory way.

Many abolitionists charge that the death penalty is disproportionately applied to African-Americans and the poor, but death penalty supporters dispute this conclusion. And the Supreme Court seems to agree with death penalty supporters. In *McCleskey v. Kemp* (1987), the Court rejected a convicted criminal's challenge to Georgia's death penalty statute—a challenge that was based primarily on a statistical study.[1] The study demonstrated that in 2,000 murder cases in Georgia during the 1970s, defendants were sentenced to death in 22 percent of cases involving African-American defendants and white victims, but in only one percent of cases involving African-American defendants and African-American victims. By contrast, defendants were sentenced to death in eight percent of cases involving white defendants and white victims but only three percent of cases involving white defendants and African-American victims.

Are these numbers enough to convince you that African-Americans were being discriminated against? In every case?

Although on their face, the raw numbers indicated a clear pattern of discrimination, the study analyzed the statistics further. The study examined 230 other factors—other than race—that could be used to explain why particular defendants received the death penalty. Once these factors were considered, the study concluded, African-American defendants were only slightly more likely (1.1 times) than white defendants to receive the death penalty. Although the case put to rest—legally speaking—the notion that the application of the death penalty is racially discriminatory, abolitionists continue to make the charge a primary basis for their criticisms of the death penalty. Therefore, death penalty supporters continue to argue that the death penalty is applied in a racially nondiscriminatory manner. The Court's opinion in *McCleskey* provides a framework for the arguments that death penalty supporters continue to find valid today.

First, the death penalty is applied according to state statutes—statutes that do not discriminate according to race. State legislatures enact death penalty laws to condemn criminals, not to condemn people of any specific race. In fact, legislatures take great lengths to ensure that death sentences are given out according to very specific, race-neutral guidelines. Like most death penalty statutes, the Georgia statute applied in *McCleskey* listed specific types of offenses for which the death penalty may be given. McCleskey's sentence was

> **Should people who have been convicted of violent crimes be allowed to appeal their death sentences if their culpability is not in doubt?**

clearly within the guidelines of the law: he was sentenced to death for shooting a police officer in the face during an armed robbery. Standing alone, either killing a police officer or killing someone during an armed robbery would serve as grounds for imposing the death penalty under the Georgia statute.

Second, while statistics might be useful in showing a general trend—that a characteristic (such as race) is present in a certain percentage of outcomes (such as death sentences)— statistics cannot prove that the factor determined the outcome in any given case. Because other African-American defendants were not sentenced to death, McCleskey could not prove that his race was the cause of his death sentence. Further, the court concluded that the circumstances of McCleskey's case indicated the likelihood that he would have been sentenced to death regardless of his race:

[H]e cannot base a constitutional claim on an argument that his case differs from other cases in which defendants did receive the death penalty. On automatic appeal, the Georgia Supreme Court found that McCleskey's death sen-

FROM THE BENCH

From *McCleskey v. Kemp*, 481 U.S. 279 (1987)

[A] statistical study performed by Professors David C. Baldus, Charles Pulaski, and George Woodworth (the Baldus study) [indicates that] in Georgia during the 1970's . . . defendants charged with killing white persons received the death penalty in 11% of the cases, but defendants charged with killing blacks received the death penalty in only 1% of the cases. [Also] 4% of the black defendants received the death penalty, as opposed to 7% of the white defendants.

Baldus also . . . found that the death penalty was assessed in 22% of the cases involving black defendants and white victims; 8% of the cases involving white defendants and white victims; 1% of the cases involving black defendants and black victims; and 3% of the cases involving white defendants and black victims. Similarly, Baldus found that prosecutors sought the death penalty in 70% of the cases involving black defendants and white victims; 32% of the cases involving white defendants and white victims; 15% of the cases involving black defendants and black victims; and 19% of the cases involving white defendants and black victims. . . .

[E]ach particular decision to impose the death penalty is made by a petit jury selected from a properly constituted venire. Each jury is unique in its composition, and the Constitution requires that its decision rest on consideration of innumerable factors that vary according to the characteristics of the individual defendant and the facts of the particular capital offense. . . .

[Georgia's death penalty] statute narrows the class of murders subject to the death penalty to cases in which the jury finds at least one statutory aggravating circumstance beyond a reasonable doubt. Conversely, it allows the defendant to introduce any relevant mitigating evidence that might influence the jury not to impose a death sentence. . . . The statute requires [the Georgia Supreme Court] to review each sentence to determine whether it was imposed under the influence of passion or prejudice, whether the evidence supports the jury's finding of a

tence was not disproportionate to other death sentences imposed in the State. . . . The court supported this conclusion with an appendix containing citations to 13 cases involving generally similar murders.[2]

statutory aggravating circumstance, and whether the sentence is disproportionate to sentences imposed in generally similar murder cases. To aid the court's review, the trial judge answers a questionnaire about the trial, including detailed questions as to "the quality of the defendant's representation [and] whether race played a role in the trial." . . .

Even Professor Baldus does not contend that his statistics prove that race enters into any capital sentencing decisions or that race was a factor in McCleskey's particular case. Statistics at most may show only a likelihood that a particular factor entered into some decisions. There is, of course, some risk of racial prejudice influencing a jury's decision in a criminal case. . . .

Because of the risk that the factor of race may enter the criminal justice process, we have engaged in "unceasing efforts" to eradicate racial prejudice from our criminal justice system. . . . Our efforts have been guided by our recognition that "the inestimable privilege of trial by jury . . . is a vital principle, underlying the whole administration of criminal justice." . . . Thus, it is the jury that is a criminal defendant's fundamental "protection of life and liberty against race or color prejudice." . . .

The capital sentencing decision requires the individual jurors to focus their collective judgment on the unique characteristics of a particular criminal defendant. It is not surprising that such collective judgments often are difficult to explain. But the inherent lack of predictability of jury decisions does not justify their condemnation. . . .

In light of the safeguards designed to minimize racial bias in the process, the fundamental value of jury trial in our criminal justice system, and the benefits that discretion provides to criminal defendants, we hold that the Baldus study does not demonstrate a constitutionally significant risk of racial bias affecting the Georgia capital sentencing process.

Many supporters of the death penalty willingly admit that all flaws cannot be eliminated from the criminal justice system. It seems inescapable that a defendant who can afford expert legal help—O.J. Simpson, for example—is less likely to be found guilty in a murder trial, and therefore less likely to be sentenced to death. But what can be done about the inescapable inequality between wealth and poverty? Professor Ernest Van Den Haag, a well-known death penalty supporter, cautions that society must not abandon its quest for justice simply because some people escape justice:

> **Which is more important—justice (punishing the guilty based on their crimes) or equality (punishing people alike for like crimes)?**
>
> **Where is the "middle ground"?**

We should not give up justice, or the death penalty, because we cannot extend it as equally to all the guilty as we wish. If we were not to punish one offender because another got away . . . we would give up justice for the sake of equality.[3]

Legal safeguards prevent the execution of the innocent.

Another reason why the Court upheld McCleskey's death sentence was that he had had ample opportunity to defend himself from the death penalty through the legal protections afforded to capital defendants. The U.S. legal system provides many safeguards for defendants charged with a capital offense. Foremost is the discretion allowed to juries:

> Discretion in the criminal justice system offers substantial benefits to the criminal defendant. Not only can a jury decline to impose the death sentence, it can decline to convict or choose to convict of a lesser offense. Whereas decisions against a defendant's interest may be reversed by the trial judge or on appeal, these discretionary exercises of leniency are final and unreviewable.

State laws also provide special protections to capital defendants. Typically, the defendant is appointed a defense team of two or more attorneys, is entitled to a sentencing hearing in front of a jury, and receives an automatic appeal if sentenced to death. As illustrated by cases such as that of Gary Cone—who in 2002 was still appealing his 1982 death sentence for a double homicide committed in 1980—condemned criminals have ample opportunity to appeal their sentences. Therefore, death penalty supporters argue, whether or not a prosecutor or a jury might have been influenced by racial animosity toward a defendant—because of either the defendant's race or the victim's race—the appeals process ensures that any such alleged discrimination can be brought up during the lengthy appeals process.

Death penalty supporters have sharply criticized the 1987 study by Radelet and Bedau that purported to show that 350 people had been wrongly convicted of capital offenses. Two attorneys with the U.S. Department of Justice published a study the following year refuting the abolitionists' analysis.[4] Of the 350 cases cited, the defendant was sentenced to death in only 139 of them, and only 23 were actually executed. And, as the authors of the original study admitted, the conclusions of innocence in these cases were based on evidence gathered outside of the judicial proceedings. Further, nobody confessed to the crimes or was convicted of the crimes that led to any of the executions.

> **What is proved by a failure to identify another person as guilty?**
>
> **Can there still be "reasonable doubt" of the convicted person's innocence?**

Death penalty supporters believe that since the death penalty was restored by the 1976 *Gregg* decision, nobody who was demonstrably innocent has been executed. While it might be true that some people are erroneously arrested for crimes that they did not commit, are charged with them, or even are convicted of them and sentenced to death, death penalty supporters argue, the lengthy and comprehensive appeals process has prevented the execution of innocent people.

FROM THE BENCH

From *Atkins v. Virginia*, Slip op. no. 00-8452 (June 20, 2002)

Given the well-known fact that anticrime legislation is far more popular than legislation providing protections for persons guilty of violent crime, the large number of States prohibiting the execution of mentally retarded persons (and the complete absence of States passing legislation reinstating the power to conduct such executions) provides powerful evidence that today our society views mentally retarded offenders as categorically less culpable than the average criminal. The evidence carries even greater force when it is noted that the legislatures that have addressed the issue have voted overwhelmingly in favor of the prohibition.

This consensus unquestionably reflects widespread judgment about the relative culpability of mentally retarded offenders, and the relationship between mental retardation and the penological purposes served by the death penalty. Additionally, it suggests that some characteristics of mental retardation undermine the strength of the procedural protections that our capital jurisprudence steadfastly guards.

As discussed above, clinical definitions of mental retardation require not only subaverage intellectual functioning, but also significant limitations in adaptive skills such as communication, self-care, and self-direction that became manifest before age 18. Mentally retarded persons frequently know the difference between right and wrong and are competent to stand trial. Because of their impairments, however, by definition they have diminished capacities to understand and process information, to communicate, to abstract from mistakes and learn from experience, to engage in logical reasoning, to control impulses, and to understand the reactions of others. There is no evidence that they are more likely to engage in criminal conduct than others, but there is abundant evidence that they often act on impulse rather than pursuant to a premeditated plan, and that in group settings they are followers rather than leaders. Their deficiencies do not warrant an exemption from criminal

The ban on executing people with mental retardation will hinder justice.

By 2002, many states had passed laws limiting or banning the execution of people with mental retardation—generally

sanctions, but they do diminish their personal culpability....

With respect to deterrence—the interest in preventing capital crimes by prospective offenders—"it seems likely that 'capital punishment can serve as a deterrent only when murder is the result of premeditation and deliberation.'"... Exempting the mentally retarded from that punishment will not affect the "cold calculus that precedes the decision" of other potential murderers....Indeed, that sort of calculus is at the opposite end of the spectrum from behavior of mentally retarded offenders. The theory of deterrence in capital sentencing is predicated upon the notion that the increased severity of the punishment will inhibit criminal actors from carrying out murderous conduct. Yet it is the same cognitive and behavioral impairments that make these defendants less morally culpable—for example, the diminished ability to understand and process information, to learn from experience, to engage in logical reasoning, or to control impulses—that also make it less likely that they can process the information of the possibility of execution as a penalty and, as a result, control their conduct based upon that information. Nor will exempting the mentally retarded from execution lessen the deterrent effect of the death penalty with respect to offenders who are not mentally retarded. Such individuals are unprotected by the exemption and will continue to face the threat of execution. Thus, executing the mentally retarded will not measurably further the goal of deterrence....

Our independent evaluation of the issue reveals no reason to disagree with the judgment of "the legislatures that have recently addressed the matter" and concluded that death is not a suitable punishment for a mentally retarded criminal. We are not persuaded that the execution of mentally retarded criminals will measurably advance the deterrent or the retributive purpose of the death penalty. Construing and applying the Eighth Amendment in the light of our "evolving standards of decency," we therefore conclude that such punishment is excessive and that the Constitution "places a substantive restriction on the State's power to take the life" of a mentally retarded offender....

Does it seem fair that a person with an IQ of 71 can be executed and a person with an IQ of 69 cannot?

That an American cannot vote even one day before his or her 18th birthday?

Are such thresholds good policy?

meaning people who score lower than 70 on standardized IQ tests. Other states did not have a similar ban, but instead allowed jurors to consider a defendant's diminished mental capacity as a "mitigating" factor that might influence them to impose a lesser sentence. However, in the case of *Atkins v. Virginia* (2002), the U.S. Supreme Court held that the execution of people with mental retardation violates the Eighth Amendment's ban on cruel and unusual punishment.

Before the Court rendered its decision, many death penalty supporters opposed a total ban—not because they supported the execution of people whose mental retardation impairs their ability to distinguish right from wrong, but because a constitutional ban would encourage questionable claims of retardation. For example, the Criminal Justice Legal Foundation filed a brief *amicus curiae* ("as a friend of the court," an "amicus brief") supporting the state of Virginia, announcing, "Our participation in this case will be to help assure that cold-blooded murderers are not able to avoid the punishment they have earned with an unsupported claim that they suffer a mental deficiency."[5] In the Atkins case itself, a clinical psychologist testifying for the prosecution had disputed the defendant's claim of mental retardation. Additionally, his crime was particularly brutal:

> After spending the day drinking alcohol and smoking marijuana, petitioner Daryl Renard Atkins and a partner in crime drove to a convenience store, intending to rob a customer. Their victim was Eric Nesbitt, an airman from Langley Air Force Base, whom they abducted, drove to a

In 2002, the Supreme Court ruled that because of his mental retardation Daryl Renard Atkins could not be executed. Many opponents of the death penalty hailed the decision as an important and long-overdue reform.

nearby automated teller machine, and forced to withdraw $200. They then drove him to a deserted area, ignoring his pleas to leave him unharmed. According to the co-conspirator, whose testimony the jury evidently credited, Atkins ordered Nesbitt out of the vehicle and, after he had taken only a few steps, shot him one, two, three, four, five, six, seven, eight times in the thorax, chest, abdomen, arms, and legs. . . . The jury also heard testimony about petitioner's 16 prior felony convictions for robbery, attempted robbery, abduction, use of a firearm, and maiming.[6]

> **Which makes more sense—allowing juries to decide whether a defendant's mental capacity is a mitigating factor or drawing a clear line to apply to all cases?**

Justice Scalia, in a dissent from the Court's holding that executing people with mental retardation violates the Constitution, wrote:

This newest invention promises to be more effective than any of the others in turning the process of capital trial into a game. . . . [T]he symptoms of this condition can readily be feigned. And whereas the capital defendant who feigns insanity risks commitment to a mental institution until he can be cured (and then tried and executed) . . . the capital defendant who feigns mental retardation risks nothing at all. The mere pendency of the present case has brought us petitions by death row inmates claiming for the first time, after multiple habeas petitions, that they are retarded.[7]

Many death penalty supporters share Justice Scalia's concern that false claims of mental retardation will clog up the court system.

Death penalty supporters believe that when similar crimes are compared, there is no pattern of racism in sentencing. Additionally, people can be sentenced to death only if convicted of a capital crime, and once convicted, the appeals process allows for overturning wrongful convictions. The Supreme Court's recent ban on executing people with mental retardation will hinder justice by encouraging false claims of retardation.

Capital Punishment Is Applied Unfairly

R egardless of the Supreme Court's 1987 decision in *McCleskey v. Kemp*, abolitionists believe that the death penalty continues to be applied in a discriminatory way. In the words of Richard Dieter, executive director of the Death Penalty Information Center, "From . . . slavery . . . through the years of lynchings and Jim Crow laws, capital punishment has always been deeply affected by race. Unfortunately, the days of racial bias in the death penalty are not a remnant of the past."[1] One of the so-called reforms of the French Revolution was that members of the upper and lower classes were executed by the same method; centuries later in the United States, the death

> The judiciary system routinely overturns verdicts and sentences based on remarks that are deemed racist, but how can it deal with lingering societal racism?

penalty is reserved almost exclusively for the poorest defendants. And although the Supreme Court recently barred the execution of people with mental retardation, abolitionists firmly believe that the most vulnerable defendants are the ones to receive the death penalty.

Race plays too large a role in sentencing.

In some cases, like Clarence Brandley's—in which a police investigator, deciding who would hang for the crime, told him, "Since you're the nigger, you're elected"—racism plays an obvious role. However, in many other cases, racism plays perhaps a subtler role. The study at issue in *McCleskey* clearly indicates that the death penalty is handed out in a way that disproportionately affects African-American defendants, as well as defendants convicted of killing white victims. More recent studies confirm this: According to the nonprofit Death Penalty Information Center, African-American defendants in Philadelphia are nearly four times as likely to receive a death sentence as are white defendants in similar cases, and nationally, 98 percent of district attorneys in counties with the death penalty are white. The organization says discrimination is common: "Examinations of [racial bias] have now been conducted in every major death penalty state. In 96% of these reviews, there was a pattern of either race-of-victim or race-of-defendant discrimination, or both."[2]

Is it fair to assume that white district attorneys are biased against African-American defendants?

Should society take active steps to increase the number of African-American district attorneys?

How can district attorneys and other officials overcome their own prejudices?

One way to eliminate racial discrepancies in sentencing, some abolitionists suggest, is to strictly limit the crimes for which the death penalty may be given. In his dissent in *McCleskey*, Justice Stevens noted:

[T]here exist certain categories of extremely serious crimes for which prosecutors consistently seek, and juries consistently impose, the death penalty without regard to the race of the victim or the race of the offender. If Georgia were to narrow the class of death-eligible defendants to those categories, the danger of arbitrary and discriminatory imposition of the death penalty would be significantly decreased, if not eradicated.[3]

Demographic characteristics of prisoners under sentence of death, 2000

| Characteristic | Prisoners under sentence of death, 2000 | | |
	Yearend	Admission	Removals
Total number under sentence of death	3,593	214	161
Gender			
Male	98.5%	96.3%	96.9%
Female	1.5	3.7	3.1
Race			
White	55.4%	57.0%	57.1%
Black	42.7	40.2	41.0
All other races*	1.9	2.8	1.9
Hispanic origin			
Hispanic	10.6%	17.0%	8.6%
Non-Hispanic	89.4	83.0	91.4
Education			
8th grade or less	14.4%	17.6%	12.7%
9th-11th grade	37.3	34.1	39.6
High school graduate/GED	38.2	39.8	40.3
Any college	10.1	8.5	7.5
Median	11th	11th	11th
Marital status			
Married	22.6%	23.5%	27.5%
Divorced/separated	21.0	18.7	25.4
Widowed	2.8	3.2	4.2
Never married	53.6	54.5	43.0

Note: Calculations are based on those cases for which data were reported. Missing data by category were as follows:

	Yearend	Admission	Removals
Hispanic origin	382	67	22
Education	490	38	27
Marital status	329	27	19

*At yearend 1999, other races consisted of 28 American Indians, 24 Asians, and 13 self-identified Hispanics. During 2000, 2 American Indians and 4 Asians were admitted; 1 American Indian, 1 Asian and 1 self-identified Hispanic were removed.

It is important to note that some death penalty supporters also favor limiting the death penalty to the most serious of crimes.

Poverty plays too large a role in sentencing.

In addition to the racist views that can—consciously or unconsciously—influence prosecutors, judges, and jurors, many abolitionists believe, like Hugo Adam Bedau, that the death penalty is tainted by "[d]iscrimination against the poor (and in our society, racial minorities are disproportionately poor)."[4] Organizations opposing the death penalty, such as the American Civil Liberties Union (ACLU), cite inadequate legal representation as a key factor in determining whether a defendant is sentenced to death in murder cases. Indigent defendants—those who cannot afford a lawyer—are entitled to legal representation; however, court-appointed lawyers are overworked and underpaid. According to the ACLU, a lawyer cannot earn a living representing indigent defendants in capital trials, and the lawyer might even *lose* money by taking the case: "In some jurisdictions the hourly rates for appointed attorneys are less than the minimum wage, and usually much less than the lawyer's hourly expenses."[5]

Normally, capital defendants have two lawyers. Would it be better for them to have one lawyer, who would be paid twice as much?

Because the pay for court-appointed lawyers is so low, and the cases require so much time to prepare adequately, many convicted defendants are sentenced to death after being represented by lawyers who are inexperienced and unprepared for the complexities of a capital trial. The ACLU criticizes the lack of funding for court-appointed defense attorneys, investigators, and expert witnesses "in the face of the almost limitless... funding for the prosecution," and concludes that the lack of funding results in a death penalty that discriminates against the poor:

> Wealthy people who can hire their own counsel are generally spared the death penalty, no matter how heinous their crimes. Poor people do not have the same opportunity to buy their lives.[6]

An example used by abolitionists to highlight the problems with court-appointed council is the case of Ronald Frye. Living in poverty and addicted to crack cocaine, Frye was appointed two lawyers to defend him from charges that he had stabbed his landlord after the landlord had notified Frye of his eviction. Frye's crime was brutal, but the jury never heard about Frye's own abusive childhood. Although Frye appealed his death sentence based on claims that his court-appointed attorneys had not represented him effectively, his appeal was denied, and the state of North Carolina executed him by lethal injection on August 31, 2001.

At Frye's trial, the defense attorneys had called an expert witness to discuss Frye's mental state. In discussions with this clinical psychologist,

Should abuse suffered during childhood factor into a convicted criminal's sentence?

What if the victim had nothing to do with that abuse?

Frye recounted a particularly troubled personal history: at the age of four, he was given away at a restaurant by his parents to a family of strangers; he was severely beaten and subjected to extreme physical torture by the father of that family; subsequently, he had lived in several foster homes. Later, as a teenager, Frye dropped out of high school and abused drugs.[7]

The psychologist testified at trial that, "Frye suffered from paranoia, mixed substance abuse, mixed personality, child abuse syndrome . . . [and a] diminished capacity to know right from wrong. . . ." However, because Frye did not want to involve his family in the trial, the defense attorneys never presented any details about Frye's being given away to strangers or being whipped with a bullwhip, or any other details of a youth filled with abuse, poverty, and drugs.

More disturbingly, one of Frye's attorneys abused alcohol throughout the time that he was representing Frye. Although the attorney later was forced to withdraw from another capital case, the federal court that heard Frye's appeal did not find the attorney's alcohol abuse grounds for overturning the death sentence:

> We are indeed troubled by [the attorney's] acknowledgment of a decades-long routine of drinking approximately twelve ounces of rum each evening. However, the district court found that [he] "never consumed alcohol during the work day and never performed any work on the case when he had consumed alcohol." . . . We agree with our sister circuits that, in order for an attorney's alcohol addiction to make his assistance constitutionally ineffective, there must be specific instances of deficient performance attributable to alcohol.[8]

Unlike the Texas inmate whose death sentence was overturned because his lawyer had slept through parts of the trial, Frye was not so lucky. Unfortunately, say death penalty opponents, most capital defendants simply do not receive adequate legal help.

Abolitionists won a victory when the Supreme Court banned the execution of people with mental retardation in *Atkins v. Virginia* (2002). Much of the court's reasoning was based on the unique challenges faced by mentally retarded defendants, such as the danger of "false confessions" and a "demeanor [that] may create an unwarranted impression of lack of remorse for their crimes." However, some of the rationales used by the court could just as easily apply to other groups. Minorities who are subject to discrimination might also have a "lesser ability . . . to make a persuasive showing of mitigation in the face of prosecutorial evidence of one or more aggravating factors." Similarly, people who lack education might also be "less able to give meaningful assistance to their counsel," and "typically [be] poor witnesses."

> **How do *Atkins* and *McCleskey* differ?**
>
> **Could the Supreme Court have made a rule that African-Americans could not be sentenced to death?**

(continued on page 84)

FROM THE BENCH

From *McCleskey v. Kemp*, 481 U.S. 279 (1987) (Brennan, J., dissenting)

At some point in this case, Warren McCleskey doubtless asked his lawyer whether a jury was likely to sentence him to die. A candid reply to this question would have been disturbing. First, counsel would have to tell McCleskey that few of the details of the crime or of McCleskey's past criminal conduct were more important than the fact that his victim was white. . . . Furthermore, counsel would feel bound to tell McCleskey that defendants charged with killing white victims in Georgia are 4.3 times as likely to be sentenced to death as defendants charged with killing blacks. . . . In addition, frankness would compel the disclosure that it was more likely than not that the race of McCleskey's victim would determine whether he received a death sentence: 6 of every 11 defendants convicted of killing a white person would not have received the death penalty if their victims had been black . . . while, among defendants with aggravating and mitigating factors comparable to McCleskey's, 20 of every 34 would not have been sentenced to die if their victims had been black. . . . Finally, the assessment would not be complete without the information that cases involving black defendants and white victims are more likely to result in a death sentence than cases featuring any other racial combination of defendant and victim. . . . The story could be told in a variety of ways, but McCleskey could not fail to grasp [that] there was a significant chance that race would play a prominent role in determining if he lived or died. . . .

The Baldus study indicates that, after taking into account some 230 non-racial factors that might legitimately influence a sentencer, the jury more likely than not would have spared McCleskey's life had his victim been black. [In cases] in which the jury has considerable discretion in choosing a sentence . . . death is imposed in 34% of white-victim crimes and 14% of black-victim crimes, a difference of 139% in the rate of imposition of the death penalty. . . . In other words, just under 59%—almost 6 in 10—defendants comparable to McCleskey would not have received the death penalty if their victims had been black.

Furthermore, even examination of the sentencing system as a whole, factoring in those cases in which the jury exercises little discretion, indicates the influence of race on capital sentencing. For the Georgia system as a whole . . .

death is imposed in 11% of all white-victim cases, [and] the rate in comparably aggravated black-victim cases is 5%. The rate of capital sentencing in a white-victim case is thus 120% greater than the rate in a black-victim case. Put another way, over half—55%—of defendants in white-victim crimes in Georgia would not have been sentenced to die if their victims had been black. Of the more than 200 variables potentially relevant to a sentencing decision, race of the victim is a powerful explanation for variation in death sentence rates—as powerful as nonracial aggravating factors such as a prior murder conviction or acting as the principal planner of the homicide.

These adjusted figures are only the most conservative indication of the risk that race will influence the death sentences of defendants in Georgia. Data unadjusted for the mitigating or aggravating effect of other factors show an even more pronounced disparity by race. The capital sentencing rate for all white-victim cases was almost 11 times greater than the rate for black-victim cases. . . . Furthermore, blacks who kill whites are sentenced to death at nearly 22 times the rate of blacks who kill blacks, and more than 7 times the rate of whites who kill blacks. . . . In addition, prosecutors seek the death penalty for 70% of black defendants with white victims, but for only 15% of black defendants with black victims, and only 19% of white defendants with black victims. . . . Since our decision upholding the Georgia capital sentencing system in [*Gregg v. Georgia*], the State has executed seven persons. All of the seven were convicted of killing whites, and six of the seven executed were black. Such execution figures are especially striking in light of the fact that, during the period encompassed by the Baldus study, only 9.2% of Georgia homicides involved black defendants and white victims, while 60.7% involved black victims. The statistical evidence in this case thus relentlessly documents the risk that McCleskey's sentence was influenced by racial considerations. This evidence shows that there is a better than even chance in Georgia that race will influence the decision to impose the death penalty: a majority of defendants in white-victim crimes would not have been sentenced to die if their victims had been black. . . . Surely, we should not be willing to take a person's life if the chance that his death sentence was irrationally imposed is more likely than not. In light of the gravity of the interest at stake, petitioner's statistics on their face are a powerful demonstration of the type of risk that our Eighth Amendment jurisprudence has consistently condemned.

(continued from page 81)

Another reason why the *Atkins* decision might give some hope to abolitionists is that the Court accepted an overall pattern of discrimination as a reason for striking down the death penalty as applied to an entire group of defendants: "Mentally retarded defendants in the aggregate face a special risk of wrongful execution." This seems to be a major change in philosophy from the *McCleskey* decision, which rejected evidence of widespread racial disparities in sentencing as a rationale for overturning McCleskey's death sentence.

Capital punishment diverts money from crime prevention.

Another way, many abolitionists argue, that the death penalty discriminates against the poor, minorities, and other vulnerable groups is that the high cost of litigating capital cases diverts money from the root causes of crime. Not only are the poor and certain minority groups more likely to be convicted of a crime, but they also are frequently victims of crime. Sadly, say abolitionists, the high costs of enforcing the death penalty—as opposed to prison sentences—mean that the criminal justice system is using resources that it could be using to fight crime. Many jurisdictions have, in fact, reduced the size of their police forces while continuing to impose the death penalty.

A report by the Death Penalty Information Center based on nationwide surveys found that even law enforcement officials—to a large extent—think that the death penalty is not working, and society should devote the millions of dollars spent each year on enforcing the death penalty to crime prevention measures. The report cites resolutions passed by various law enforcement and anti-crime organizations:

> Rarely is the death penalty even mentioned in their discussions. Instead, the solutions are changes and programs that affect a broad range of people and go to the roots of why violent crime has become so prevalent.[9]

Among the crime prevention techniques cited by the study as being more effective than the death penalty in reducing crime were: increased numbers of police officers; "community policing," including more officers on foot patrol; offering drug treatment programs to anyone who needs them; creating separate drug courts to handle minor offenses; address-ing family violence; reducing high school dropout rates; teaching conflict resolution skills in schools; reducing unemploy-ment; enacting tougher anti-gang laws; and removing illegal handguns from the streets.

> **Which is the best use of public funding: the death penalty, more police, or crime prevention programs?**

Abolitionists firmly believe that the death penalty is adminis-tered in a racist manner: African-American defendants, and all other defendants who kill white people, are much more likely to be sentenced to death. Poverty is another factor in the unfairness of the death penalty; poor people are appointed lawyers who are too overworked and under-prepared to effectively represent their clients. Millions of dollars are spent on the death penalty instead of on social programs that could help to prevent crime.

The Future of Capital Punishment in America

What is the future of the death penalty in the United States? Almost everyone—supporters and opponents—agrees that the current system is broken. However, people disagree about how to fix it. Many people think that the answer is to eliminate the death penalty entirely, but others believe that we should remove some of the barriers to execution. While many people have strongly held beliefs about the death penalty, many Americans are not so sure how they feel—national opinion polls often produce conflicting results.

> **Should the current system continue—in which the Supreme Court widens or narrows the availability of the death penalty through its decisions— or should the U.S. Congress intervene?**

On the one hand, a majority will answer "yes" if asked whether they support capital punishment. On the other hand, far fewer people answer affirmatively if they are asked whether they would support the death penalty if murderers could instead be sentenced to life in prison with absolutely no chance of parole.

Support for the death penalty remains high—especially at election time—and many politicians fear taking a strong stand against capital punishment. Abolitionists continue to try to influence public opinion through traditional attacks on the death penalty, such as that it does not deter crime, that innocent people are sentenced to death, and that the death penalty is given disproportionately to the poor and minorities. Increasingly, however, abolitionists seek to educate the public about the existence of laws allowing for life in prison without parole, reasoning that a major reason for public support of the death penalty is that many people are under the impression that murderers who are sentenced to prison will—like Willie Horton—be released a few years later and commit more crimes. Whatever a person's position on the death penalty, most people argue that our nation must find some way to reduce crime rates, and debates often look at ways of changing how the death penalty is administered.

Possible Changes to the Death Penalty in the United States

Despite majority support for the death penalty, many dedicated opponents remain vigorously dedicated to the cause of abolishing the death penalty in the United States. The death penalty could be abolished in several ways: crime by crime (for example, rape is no longer grounds for the death penalty), state by state (a third of states have already abolished the death penalty), or class by class

> **Should the number of crimes punishable by death be limited?**
>
> **Which types of crime should be punished the most severely?**

(such as abolishing the death penalty for minors). Of course, the ultimate goal of abolitionists is for the United States to join other

Capital offenses, by State, 2000

Alabama. Intentional murder with 18 aggravating factors (13A-5-40(a)(1)-(18)).

Arizona. First-degree murder accompanied by at least 1 of 10 aggravating factors (A.R.S 13-703(F)).

Arkansas. Capital murder (Ark. Code Ann. 5-10-101) with a finding of at least 1 of 10 aggravating circumstances; treason. Capital sentencing excludes persons found to be mentally retarded.

California. First-degree murder with special circumstances; train wrecking; treason; perjury causing execution.

Colorado. First-degree murder with at least 1 of 15 aggravating factors; treason. Capital sentencing excludes persons determined to be mentally retarded.

Connecticut. Capital felony with 9 categories of aggravated homicide (C.G.S. 53a-54b).

Delaware. First-degree murder with aggravating circumstances.

Florida. First-degree murder; felony murder; capital drug trafficking; capital sexual battery.

Georgia. Murder; kidnaping with bodily injury or ransom when the victim dies; aircraft hijacking; treason.

Idaho. First-degree murder with aggravating factors; aggravated kidnaping.

Illinois. First-degree murder with 1 of 15 aggravating circumstances.

Indiana. Murder with 16 aggravating circumstances (IC 35-50-2-9). Capital sentencing excludes persons determined to be mentally retarded.

Kansas. Capital murder with 7 aggravating circumstances (KSA 21-3439). Capital sentencing excludes persons determined to be mentally retarded.

Kentucky. Murder with aggravating factors; kidnaping with aggravating factors (KRS 532.025).

Louisiana. First-degree murder; aggravated rape of victim under age 12; treason (La. R.S. 14:30, 14:42, and 14:113).

Maryland. First-degree murder, either premeditated or during the commission of a felony, provided that certain death eligibility requirements are satisfied.

Mississippi. Capital murder (97-3-19(2) MCA); aircraft piracy (97-25-55(1) MCA).

Missouri. First-degree murder (565.020 RSMO 1994).

Montana. Capital murder with 1 of 9 aggravating circumstances (46-18-303 MCA); capital sexual assault (45-5-503 MCA).

Nebraska. First-degree murder with a finding of at least 1 statutorily-defined aggravating circumstance.

Nevada. First-degree murder with 14 aggravating circumstances.

New Hampshire. Six categories of capital murder (RSA 630:1, RSA 630:5).

New Jersey. Knowing/purposeful murder by one's own conduct; contract murder; solicitation by command or threat in furtherance of a narcotics conspiracy (NJSA 2C:11-3C).

New Mexico. First-degree murder with at least 1 of 7 statutorily-defined aggravating circumstances (Section 30-2-1 A, NMSA).

New York. First-degree murder with 1 of 12 aggravating factors. Capital sentencing excludes mentally retarded persons.

North Carolina. First-degree murder (NCGS §14-17).

Ohio. Aggravated murder with at least 1 of 9 aggravating circumstances. (O.R.C. secs. 2903.01, 2929.02, and 2929.04).

Oklahoma. First-degree murder in conjunction with a finding of at least 1 of 8 statutorily defined aggravating circumstances.

Oregon. Aggravated murder (ORS 163.095).

Pennsylvania. First-degree murder with 18 aggravating circumstances.

South Carolina. Murder with 1 of 10 aggravating circumstances (§ 16-3-20(C)(a)). Mental retardation is a mitigating factor.

South Dakota. First-degree murder with 1 of 10 aggravating circumstances; aggravated kidnaping.

Tennessee. First-degree murder with 1 of 14 aggravating circumstances.

Texas. Criminal homicide with 1 of 8 aggravating circumstances (TX Penal Code 19.03).

Utah. Aggravated murder (76-5-202, Utah Code annotated).

Virginia. First-degree murder with 1 of 12 aggravating circumstances (VA Code § 18.2-31).

Washington. Aggravated first-degree murder.

Wyoming. First-degree murder.

Western industrialized nations in abolishing the death penalty completely. But in order to partially or completely abolish the death penalty, opponents must influence public opinion.

Abolition could be achieved either through the legislature or through the courts. Either way depends on a major shift in public opinion away from support of the death penalty. The U.S. Supreme Court has consistently relied upon "currently prevailing standards of decency" in determining whether a particular application of the death penalty violates the Eighth Amendment's prohibition of cruel and unusual punishment. For example, prevailing attitudes about executing people with mental retardation served as a basis for prohibiting the practice. Certainly, state legislatures will not abolish the death penalty unless public opinion shifts away from support of capital punishment, because politicians depend on votes, and death penalty supporters actively campaign against candidates who oppose capital punishment or want to limit its use.

Reducing the number of crimes for which the death penalty can be given is an approach that has found support from abolitionists, death penalty proponents, and supporters of racial justice. It is thought that limiting the death penalty to the most serious and shocking of crimes would eliminate juries' discretion, which often leads to more African-American defendants, and more murderers of white victims, being sentenced to death. Rather than executing a miniscule percentage of the people who commit potentially capital crimes, stricter guidelines would allow for executing a large percentage of people who are convicted of the worst types of crimes. However, the question that remains about this approach—for people who believe that the death penalty is a deterrent—is how to deter those crimes that would no longer be punishable by death.

Perhaps the answer of how to deter those crimes—or even how to deter the most heinous crimes—is to consistently enforce sentences of life in prison without parole. One of the advantages of such sentences is that it actually costs less (according to many estimates) to imprison someone for life than it does to pay for the legal process and the death row incarceration of someone sentenced to death. Without the extra considerations of leniency given to capital defendants and the endless appeals process, the life-without-parole sentences could be enforced more consistently. If criminals knew that being caught for a crime would mean that they would never regain their freedom, they might be more deterred than they would be by a slight chance that they would be executed.

> **How does the alternative of life in prison without parole affect the idea of the death penalty?**

Of course, a sentence of life without parole does not accomplish the same level of retribution—a result that some victims' families might feel is unfair. Perhaps the answer is to do more for victims' families. Many states have fairly comprehensive victims' rights laws. One possibility for improvement is to require convicted criminals to provide restitution, thus obligating them to work while in prison for life.

International Comparisons

Death penalty opponents frequently compare U.S. homicide rates to those of the United Kingdom, which are much lower despite the fact that the British have abolished the death penalty. However, Saudi Arabia, which also has very low crime rates, executes even more people than the United States does, executing people much sooner and using the spectacle of public beheading as a warning to would-be criminals. It is difficult to draw any conclusions from comparing the United States to the United Kingdom and Saudi Arabia because their laws and cultures are so different from those of the U.S.

The United Kingdom and other Western nations that have abolished the death penalty also have much stricter limits on gun ownership. Saudi Arabia and other countries that execute more people than the United States, such as China and

Iraq, do not have the same human rights protections—or decades-long appeals process—as the United States. But Americans seem unlikely to want to part with either the right to bear arms or their civil liberties.

Perhaps the answer to U.S. crime rates has nothing to do with the death penalty. Many believe that gun control, drug treatment, better schools, and other social programs are much more effective than the death penalty in reducing crime. These programs can be instituted regardless of what type of action is taken on the death penalty. Other nations have lowered their crime rates whether or not they use the death penalty as a tool. The question of how to reduce crime remains a major challenge for scholars, law enforcement officials, and everyday citizens. An ideal solution would be for the United States to reduce crime to the point that the death penalty is no longer needed—but this goal is far from realization.

> **Are other nations' crime rates useful for making decisions in the United States, or is the U.S. too different from other nations for their problems to be relevant?**

Despite the high costs and questionable effects of the death penalty, public support remains strong in the absence of other solutions for deterring crime and assisting crime victims and their families. Internationally, other Western industrialized nations have abolished the death penalty, but the United States has a much higher crime rate than these nations and is still seeking an answer to reducing crime rates.

What Is Capital Punishment?

1 Harry Henderson, *Capital Punishment* (Facts on File, 2000), 6.

2 Jason DeParle, "Willie Going to Chair as Proud Man," *New Orleans Times-Picayune* (27 December 1984).

3 Helen Prejean, *Dead Man Walking* (Random House, 1993), 128.

4 Helen Prejean, *Dead Man Walking* (Random House, 1993), 210–211.

5 Helen Prejean, *Dead Man Walking* (Random House, 1993), 213.

6 Jason DeParle, "Victim's Parents Watch Willie Die," *New Orleans Times-Picayune* (28 December 1984).

7 Helen Prejean, *Dead Man Walking* (Random House, 1993), 213.

8 Rev. Jesse L. Jackson, Sr. and Representative Jesse L. Jackson, Jr., *Legal Lynching: Racism, Injustice & the Death Penalty* (Marlowe & Co., 1996), 57.

9 Pope John Paul II, *Evangelium Vitae,* Encyclical Letter (March 25, 1995).

Point: The Death Penalty Is an Effective Deterrent to Crime

1 *Gregg v. Georgia,* 428 U.S. 153, 185 (1976) (plurality opinion).

2 American Bar Association: Division for Public Education, "The Death Penalty: Purposes of the Death Penalty," *Focus on Law Studies* 12:2 (Spring 1997). Available online at *www.abanet.org/publiced/focus/spr97pur.html.*

3 Isaac Ehrlich, "The Deterrent Effect of Capital Punishment—A Question of Life and Death," *American Economic Review* 65:3 (June 1975), 397–417.

4 *Furman v. Georgia,* 408 U.S. 238, 253 (1972) (Douglas, J., concurring).

5 Alan I. Bigel, *Justices William J. Brennan, Jr. and Thurgood Marshall on Capital Punishment: Its Constitutionality, Morality, Deterrent Effect, and Interpretation by the Court* (University Press of America, 1997), 44. Citing Frank G. Carrington, *Neither Cruel Nor Unusual* (1978).

6 Arlen Specter, "A Swifter Death Penalty Would Be an Effective Deterrent," in *Human Events* (15 July 1995).

Counterpoint: The Death Penalty Is Not an Effective Deterrent to Crime

1 Thorsten Sellin, *The Death Penalty: A Report for the Model Penal Code Project of the American Law Institute (ALI),* 1959.

2 Thorsten Sellin, *Capital Punishment,* Harper & Row, 1967.

3 *Gregg v. Georgia,* 428 U.S. 153, 235–236 (1976) (Marshall, J., dissenting).

4 Rev. Jesse L. Jackson, Sr. and Representative Jesse L. Jackson, Jr., *Legal Lynching: Racism, Injustice & the Death Penalty* (Marlowe & Co., 1996), 124.

5 Richard Rhodes, *Why They Kill: The Discoveries of a Maverick Criminologist* (Alfred A. Knopf, 1999), 88–89.

6 Michael Kroenenwatter, *Capital Punishment: A Reference Handbook* (ABL-CLIO, Inc., 2001), 27.

7 Shirley Dicks, ed. *Congregation of the Condemned: Voices Against the Death Penalty* (Prometheus Books, 1991), 75.

8 *Bell v. Cone,* Slip op. no. 01-400 (May 28, 2002).

9 Shirley Dicks, ed. *Congregation of the Condemned: Voices Against the Death Penalty* (Prometheus Books, 1991), 77.

10 *Atkins v. Virginia,* Slip op. no. 00-8452 (June 20, 2002).

11 William J. Bowers and Glenn Pierce, "Deterrence or Brutalization: What Is the Effect of Executions?" *Crime and Delinquency* (1980), 26.

12 Michael Kroenenwetter, *Capital Punishment: A Reference Handbook* (ABL-CLIO, 2001), 31.

13 Michael Kroenenwetter, *Capital Punishment: A Reference Handbook* (ABL-CLIO, 2001), 33.

14 Rev. Jesse L. Jackson, Sr. and Representative Jesse L. Jackson, Jr., *Legal Lynching: Racism, Injustice & the Death Penalty* (Marlowe & Co., 1996), 126.

Point: Streamlining Capital Punishment Would Make It More Effective

1 Richard C. Dieter, "Millions Misspent: What Politicians Don't Say About the High Costs of the Death Penalty" in *The Death Penalty in America: Current Controversies*, ed. Hugo A. Bedau (Oxford University Press, 1997), 407.

2 Richard C. Dieter, "Millions Misspent: What Politicians Don't Say About the High Costs of the Death Penalty" in *The Death Penalty in America: Current Controversies*, ed. Hugo A. Bedau (Oxford University Press, 1997), 402.

3 Alex Kozinski and Sean Gallagher, "For an Honest Death Penalty," *New York Times* (8 March 1995).

3 *Dawson v. Delaware*, 503 U.S. 159, 162–163, 166 (1992).

4 *Dawson v. Delaware*, 503 U.S. 159, 170, 174–175 (1992) (Thomas, J., dissenting).

5 *Bell v. Cone*, Slip op. no. 01-400 (May 28, 2002).

Counterpoint: It Is Already Too Easy to Convict and Execute People

1 *Booth v. Maryland*, 482 U.S. 496, 499–500 (1987).

2 *Booth v. Maryland*, 482 U.S. 496, 508 (1987).

3 *Payne v. Tennessee*, 501 U.S. 808, 859–860 (1991) (Stevens, J., dissenting).

4 *Witherspoon v. Illinois*, 391 U.S. 510, 516–517 (1968).

5 *Witherspoon v. Illinois*, 391 U.S. 510, 517 (1968).

6 Clay S. Conrad, "Are You 'Death Qualified'?" *Cato Institute Daily Dispatch* (10 August 2000). See *www.cato.org*.

7 Michael L. Radelet, Hugo Adam Bedau, and Constance L. Putnam, *In Spite of Innocence: Erroneous Convictions in Capital Cases* (Northeastern University Press, 1992), 121.

8 Rev. Jesse L. Jackson, Sr. and Representative Jesse L. Jackson, Jr., *Legal Lynching: Racism, Injustice, and the Death Penalty* (Marlowe & Co., 1996), 62.

9 Hugo Adam Bedau and Michael Radelet, "Miscarriages of Justice in Potentially Capital Cases," *Stanford Law Review* 40:21, 1987.

Point: Capital Punishment Is a Just Process

1 David C. Baldus, George Woodworth, and Charles Pulaski Jr., "Comparative Review of Death Sentence: An Empirical Study of Georgia Experience," *Journal of Criminal Law and Criminology* 74, 1983.

2 *McCleskey v. Kemp*, 481 U.S. 279, 306 (1987).

3 Ernest Van Den Haag, "The Death Penalty Once More," in *The Death Penalty in America: Current Controversies*, ed. Hugo Adam Bedau (Oxford University Press, 1997), 449.

4 Stephen J. Markman and Paul G. Cassell, "Protecting the Innocent: A Response to the Bedau-Radelet Study," *Stanford Law Review* 41:1, November 1988.

5 Criminal Justice Legal Foundation, Press Release (24 September 2001).

6 *Atkins v. Virginia*, Slip op. no. 00-8452 (June 20, 2002) (Scalia, J., dissenting).

7 *Atkins v. Virginia*, Slip op. no. 00-8452 (June 20, 2002) (Scalia, J., dissenting).

Counterpoint: Capital Punishment Is Applied Unfairly

1 Richard C. Dieter, *The Death Penalty in Black & White: Who Lives, Who Dies, Who Decides* (Death Penalty Information Center, 1998).

2 Richard C. Dieter, *The Death Penalty in Black & White: Who Lives, Who Dies, Who Decides* (Death Penalty Information Center, 1998).

3 *McCleskey v. Kemp*, 481 U.S. 279, 367 (1987) (Stevens, J., dissenting).

4 Hugo Adam Bedau, "The Case Against the Death Penalty." See *www.aclu.org*.

93

5 American Civil Liberties Union, *Briefing Paper: The Death Penalty*, no. 14 (Spring 1999), 1.

6 American Civil Liberties Union, *Briefing Paper: The Death Penalty*, no. 14 (Spring 1999), 1.

7 *Frye v. Lee*, Slip op. no. CA-99-108-5-T (4th Cir., December 22, 2000).

8 *Frye v. Lee*, Slip op. no. CA-99-108-5-T (4th Cir., December 22, 2000).

9 Richard C. Dieter, *On the Front Line: Law Enforcement Views on the Death Penalty* (Death Penalty Information Center, 1995).

General Resources

Bigel, Alan I. *Justices William J. Brennan, Jr. and Thurgood Marshall on Capital Punishment: Its Constitutionality, Morality, Deterrent Effect, and Interpretation by the Court.* University Press of America, 1997.

Henderson, Harry. *Capital Punishment.* Facts on File, 2000.

Kroenenwetter, Michael. *Capital Punishment: A Reference Handbook.* ABL-CLIO, 2001.

Rhodes, Richard. *Why They Kill: The Discoveries of a Maverick Criminologist.* Alfred A. Knopf, 1999.

Wolf, Robert V. *Capital Punishment.* Chelsea House Publishers, 1997.

Supporting Capital Punishment

Ehrlich, Isaac. "The Deterrent Effect of Capital Punishment—A Question of Life and Death." *American Economic Review* 65:3 (June 1975), 397–417.

Specter, Arlen. "A Swifter Death Penalty Would Be an Effective Deterrent." *Human Events* (15 July 1995).

Kozinski, Alex, and Sean Gallagher. "For an Honest Death Penalty." *The New York Times* (8 March 1995).

Van Den Haag, Ernest. "The Death Penalty Once More." In *The Death Penalty in America: Current Controversies*, ed. Hugo Adam Bedau. Oxford University Press, 1997.

The Criminal Justice Legal Foundation
www.cjlf.org
Nonprofit legal organization supporting victims' rights and swift justice over excessive protections for the criminally accused. Information and legal arguments about current cases.

Justice For All
www.prodeathpenalty.com and *www.jfa.net*
Organization advocating for criminal justice reform to protect innocent people's lives and property. Information about scheduled executions and extensive collection of essays and articles.

The Washington Legal Foundation
www.wlf.org
Nonprofit legal organization advocating for various conservative causes, including military defense, business rights, and criminal justice reform. Plainly written summaries of recent litigation.

Against Capital Punishment

Dicks, Shirley, ed. *Congregation of the Condemned: Voices Against the Death Penalty.* Prometheus Books, 1991.

Dieter, Richard C. "Millions Misspent: What Politicians Don't Say About the High Costs of the Death Penalty." In *The Death Penalty in America: Current Controversies,* ed. Hugo A. Bedau. Oxford University Press, 1997.

_____ . *On the Front Line: Law Enforcement Views on the Death Penalty.* Death Penalty Information Center, 1995.

_____ . *The Death Penalty in Black & White: Who Lives, Who Dies, Who Decides.* Death Penalty Information Center, 1998.

Jackson, Jesse L., Sr., and Jesse L. Jackson, Jr. *Legal Lynching: Racism, Injustice & the Death Penalty.* Marlowe & Co., 1996.

Prejean, Helen. *Dead Man Walking.* Random House, 1993.

Radelet, Michael L., Hugo Adam Bedau, and Constance L. Putnam. *In Spite of Innocence: Erroneous Convictions in Capital Cases.* Northeastern University Press, 1992.

The Death Penalty Information Center
www.deathpenaltyinfo.org
Nonprofit organization that educates the public and the media about anti–death penalty viewpoints. In-depth reports and information about current cases.

The National Coalition to Abolish the Death Penalty
www.ncadp.org
National organization working to abolish the death penalty through legal and legislative advocacy at the local, state, and federal levels. Concise fact sheets and statistics about executions.

Amnesty International
www.amnesty.org
International human rights organization advocating for the abolition of the death penalty worldwide. Extensive information about the death penalty, including international comparisons.

The American Civil Liberties Union
www.aclu.org
National organization defending individual rights such as free speech, abortion, and rights in the criminal justice system. Practical information about working to abolish the death penalty.

Legislation and Case Law

Witherspoon v. Illinois, 391 U.S. 510, 516–17 (1968)
A court cannot exclude potential jurors simply for expressing general objections to capital punishment.

Furman v. Georgia, 408 U.S. 238 (1972)
Created a moratorium on capital punishment in the United States by determining that the death sentence in the case before the trial court represented cruel and unusual punishment in violation of the Eighth Amendment.

Gregg v. Georgia, 428 U.S. 153 (1976)
Capital punishment does not violate the Eighth Amendment when the law sets clear standards that guide juries in deciding whether to impose the death penalty.

McCleskey v. Kemp, 481 U.S. 279 (1987)
A study showing that in Georgia black defendants were statistically more likely to be sentenced to death than white defendants did not invalidate Georgia's death penalty stature because the statistics did not establish a violation of any specific defendant's constitutional rights.

Booth v. Maryland, 482 U.S. 496 (1987)
The use of "victim impact statements" in the sentencing phase of a capital trial unfairly prejudices the jury and therefore violates the Eighth Amendment.

Payne v. Tennessee, 501 U.S. 808 (1991)
Overruled *Booth*, holding that the use of victim impact statements is permissible to counteract a defendant's introduction of character evidence.

Dawson v. Delaware, 503 U.S. 159 (1992)
Introducing evidence at a capital trial of a defendant's membership in a racist gang unfairly influenced the jury and therefore violated the defendant's constitutional right to due process of law.

Federal Death Penalty Act of 1994, 18 U.S.C. § 3591 (2000)
Lists some of the offenses for which a federal court may impose the death penalty, including certain drug offenses. (Each state that authorizes the death penalty has a unique statute covering the punishment.)

Antiterrorism and Effective Death Penalty Act of 1996, 28 U.S.C. §§2261–2266 (2000)
Limits use of habeas corpus procedure to appeal state-imposed death sentences in federal court.

Frye v. Lee, Slip op. no. CA–99–108–5–T (4th Cir., December 22, 2000)
Despite the defense lawyer's heavy drinking during the time period of the trial, the defendant's death sentence was upheld due to lack of specific evidence that the lawyer failed to represent the defendant effectively.

Federal laws providing for the death penalty, 2000

8 U.S.C. 1342 — Murder related to the smuggling of aliens.

18 U.S.C. 32-34 — Destruction of aircraft, motor vehicles, or related facilities resulting in death.

18 U.S.C. 36 — Murder committed during a drug-related drive-by shooting.

18 U.S.C. 37 — Murder committed at an airport serving international civil aviation.

18 U.S.C. 115(b)(3) [by cross-reference to 18 U.S.C. 1111] — Retaliatory murder of a member of the immediate family of law enforcement officials.

18 U.S.C. 241, 242, 245, 247 — Civil rights offenses resulting in death.

18 U.S.C. 351 [by cross-reference to 18 U.S.C. 1111] — Murder of a member of Congress, an important executive official, or a Supreme Court Justice.

18 U.S.C. 794 — Espionage.

18 U.S.C. 844(d), (f), (i) — Death resulting from offenses involving transportation of explosives, destruction of government property, or destruction of property related to foreign or interstate commerce.

18 U.S.C. 924(i) — Murder committed by the use of a firearm during a crime of violence or a drug-trafficking crime.

18 U.S.C. 930 — Murder committed in a Federal Government facility.

18 U.S.C. 1091 — Genocide.

18 U.S.C. 1111 — First-degree murder.

18 U.S.C. 1114 — Murder of a Federal judge or law enforcement official.

18 U.S.C. 1116 — Murder of a foreign official.

18 U.S.C. 1118 — Murder by a Federal prisoner.

18 U.S.C. 1119 — Murder of a U.S. national in a foreign country.

18 U.S.C. 1120 — Murder by an escaped Federal prisoner already sentenced to life imprisonment.

18 U.S.C. 1121 — Murder of a State or local law enforcement official or other person aiding in a Federal investigation; murder of a State correctional officer.

18 U.S.C. 1201 — Murder during a kidnaping.

18 U.S.C. 1203 — Murder during a hostage taking.

18 U.S.C. 1503 — Murder of a court officer or juror.

18 U.S.C. 1512 — Murder with the intent of preventing testimony by a witness, victim, or informant.

18 U.S.C. 1513 — Retaliatory murder of a witness, victim, or informant.

18 U.S.C. 1716 — Mailing of injurious articles with intent to kill or resulting in death.

18 U.S.C. 1751 [by cross-reference to 18 U.S.C. 1111] — Assassination or kidnaping resulting in the death of the President or Vice President.

18 U.S.C. 1958 — Murder for hire.

18 U.S.C. 1959 — Murder involved in a racketeering offense.

18 U.S.C. 1992 — Willful wrecking of a train resulting in death.

18 U.S.C. 2113 — Bank-robbery-related murder or kidnaping.

18 U.S.C. 2119 — Murder related to a carjacking.

18 U.S.C. 2245 — Murder related to rape or child molestation.

18 U.S.C. 2251 — Murder related to sexual exploitation of children.

18 U.S.C. 2280 — Murder committed during an offense against maritime navigation.

18 U.S.C. 2281 — Murder committed during an offense against a maritime fixed platform.

18 U.S.C. 2332 — Terrorist murder of a U.S. national in another country.

18 U.S.C. 2332a — Murder by the use of a weapon of mass destruction.

18 U.S.C. 2340 — Murder involving torture.

18 U.S.C. 2381 — Treason.

21 U.S.C. 848(e) — Murder related to a continuing criminal enterprise or related murder of a Federal, State, or local law enforcement officer.

49 U.S.C. 1472-1473 — Death resulting from aircraft hijacking.

Bell v. Cone, Slip op. no. 01–400 (May 28, 2002)
Upheld death sentence of Vietnam veteran whose lawyer did not call any witnesses or give a closing argument during the sentencing phase of the trial to support the defendant's claims of post-traumatic stress disorder (PTSD) and drug abuse.

Atkins v. Virginia, Slip op. no. 00–8452 (June 20, 2002)
Executing people who are mentally retarded is cruel and unusual punishment in violation of the Eight Amendment.

Concepts and Standards

habeas corpus

ineffective assistance of counsel

retribution/deterrence

cruel and unusual punishment

victim impact statement

victims' rights laws

eye for an eye

death qualification

Beginning Legal Research

The goal of POINT/COUNTERPOINT is not only to provide the reader with an introduction to a controversial issue affecting society, but also to encourage the reader to explore the issue more fully. This appendix, then, is meant to serve as a guide to the reader in researching the current state of the law as well as exploring some of the public-policy arguments as to why existing laws should be changed or new laws are needed.

Like many types of research, legal research has become much faster and more accessible with the invention of the Internet. This appendix discusses some of the best starting points, but of course "surfing the Net" will uncover endless additional sources of information—some more reliable than others. Some important sources of law are not yet available on the Internet, but these can generally be found at the larger public and university libraries. Librarians usually are happy to point patrons in the right direction.

The most important source of law in the United States is the Constitution. Originally enacted in 1787, the Constitution outlines the structure of our federal government and sets limits on the types of laws that the federal government and state governments can pass. Through the centuries, a number of amendments have been added to or changed in the Constitution, most notably the first ten amendments, known collectively as the Bill of Rights, which guarantee important civil liberties. Each state also has its own constitution, many of which are similar to the U.S. Constitution. It is important to be familiar with the U.S. Constitution because so many of our laws are affected by its requirements. State constitutions often provide protections of individual rights that are even stronger than those set forth in the U.S. Constitution.

Within the guidelines of the U.S. Constitution, Congress—both the House of Representatives and the Senate—passes bills that are either vetoed or signed into law by the President. After the passage of the law, it becomes part of the United States Code, which is the official compilation of federal laws. The state legislatures use a similar process, in which bills become law when signed by the state's governor. Each state has its own official set of laws, some of which are published by the state and some of which are published by commercial publishers. The U.S. Code and the state codes are an important source of legal research; generally, legislators make efforts to make the language of the law as clear as possible.

However, reading the text of a federal or state law generally provides only part of the picture. In the American system of government, after the legislature passes laws and the executive (U.S. President or state governor) signs them, it is up to the judicial branch of the government, the court system, to interpret the laws and decide whether they violate any provision of the Constitution. At the state level, each state's supreme court has the ultimate authority in determining what a law means and whether or not it violates the state constitution. However, the federal courts—headed by the U.S. Supreme Court—can review state laws and court decisions to determine whether they violate federal laws or the U.S. Constitution. For example, a state court may find that a particular criminal law is valid under the state's constitution, but a federal court may then review the state court's decision and determine that the law is invalid under the U.S. Constitution.

It is important, then, to read court decisions when doing legal research. The Constitution uses language that is intentionally very general—for example, prohibiting "unreasonable searches and seizures" by the police—and court cases often provide more guidance. For example, the U.S. Supreme Court's 2001 decision in *Kyllo v. United States* held that scanning the outside of a person's house using a heat sensor to determine whether the person is growing marijuana is unreasonable—*if* it is done without a search warrant secured from a judge. Supreme Court decisions provide the most definitive explanation of the law of the land, and it is therefore important to include these in research. Often, when the Supreme Court has not decided a case on a particular issue, a decision by a federal appeals court or a state supreme court can provide guidance; but just as laws and constitutions can vary from state to state, so can federal courts be split on a particular interpretation of federal law or the U.S. Constitution. For example, federal appeals courts in Louisiana and California may reach opposite conclusions in similar cases.

Lawyers and courts refer to statutes and court decisions through a formal system of citations. Use of these citations reveals which court made the decision (or which legislature passed the statute) and when and enables the reader to locate the statute or court case quickly in a law library. For example, the legendary Supreme Court case *Brown v. Board of Education* has the legal citation 347 U.S. 483 (1954). At a law library, this 1954 decision can be found on page 483 of volume 347 of the U.S. Reports, the official collection of the Supreme Court's decisions. Citations can also be helpful in locating court cases on the Internet.

Understanding the current state of the law leads only to a partial understanding of the issues covered by the POINT/COUNTERPOINT series. For a fuller understanding of the issues, it is necessary to look at public-policy arguments that the current state of the law is not adequately addressing the issue. Many groups lobby for new legislation or changes to existing legislation; the National Rifle Association (NRA), for example, lobbies Congress and the state legislatures constantly to make existing gun control laws less restrictive and not to pass additional laws. The NRA and other groups dedicated to various causes might also intervene in pending court cases: a group such as Planned Parenthood might file a brief *amicus curiae* (as "a friend of the court")—called an "amicus brief"—in a lawsuit that could affect abortion rights. Interest groups also use the media to influence public opinion, issuing press releases and frequently appearing in interviews on news programs and talk shows. The books in POINT/COUNTERPOINT list some of the interest groups that are active in the issue at hand, but in each case there are countless other groups working at the local, state, and national levels. It is important to read everything with a critical eye, for sometimes interest groups present information in a way that can be read only to their advantage. The informed reader must always look for bias.

Finding sources of legal information on the Internet is relatively simple thanks to "portal" sites such as FindLaw (*www.findlaw.com*), which provides access to a variety of constitutions, statutes, court opinions, law review articles, news articles, and other resources—including all Supreme Court decisions issued since 1893. Other useful sources of information include the U.S. Government Printing Office (*www.gpo.gov*), which contains a complete copy of the U.S. Code, and the Library of Congress's THOMAS system (*thomas.loc.gov*), which offers access to bills pending before Congress as well as recently passed laws. Of course, the Internet changes every second of every day, so it is best to do some independent searching. Most cases, studies, and opinions that are cited or referred to in public debate can be found online— and *everything* can be found in one library or another.

The Internet can provide a basic understanding of most important legal issues, but not all sources can be found there. To find some documents it is necessary to visit the law library of a university or a public law library; some cities have public law libraries, and many library systems keep legal documents at the main branch. On the following page are some common citation forms.

COMMON CITATION FORMS

Source of Law	Sample Citation	Notes
U.S. Supreme Court	*Employment Division v. Smith*, 485 U.S. 660 (1988)	The U.S. Reports is the official record of Supreme Court decisions. There is also an unofficial Supreme Court ("S.Ct.") reporter.
U.S. Court of Appeals	*United States v. Lambert*, 695 F.2d 536 (11th Cir.1983)	Appellate cases appear in the Federal Reporter, designated by "F." The 11th Circuit has jurisdiction in Alabama, Florida, and Georgia.
U.S. District Court	*Carillon Importers, Ltd. v. Frank Pesce Group, Inc.*, 913 F.Supp. 1559 (S.D.Fla.1996)	Federal trial-level decisions are reported in the Federal Supplement ("F.Supp."). Some states have multiple federal districts; this case originated in the Southern District of Florida.
U.S. Code	Thomas Jefferson Commemoration Commission Act, 36 U.S.C., §149 (2002).	Sometimes the popular names of legislation—names with which the public may be familiar—are included with the U.S. Code citation.
State Supreme Court	*Sterling v. Cupp*, 290 Ore. 611, 614, 625 P.2d 123, 126 (1981)	The Oregon Supreme Court decision is reported in both the state's reporter and the Pacific regional reporter.
State statute	Pennsylvania Abortion Control Act of 1982, 18 Pa. Cons. Stat. 3203-3220 (1990)	States use many different citation formats for their statutes.

105

ABOUT THE AUTHOR

ALAN MARZILLI, of Durham, North Carolina, is an independent consultant working on several ongoing projects for state and federal government agencies and nonprofit organizations. He has spoken about mental health issues in over twenty states, the District of Columbia, and Puerto Rico; his work includes training mental health administrators, nonprofit management and staff, and people with mental illness and their family members on a wide variety of topics, including effective advocacy, community-based mental health services, and housing. He has written several handbooks and training curricula that are used nationally. He managed statewide and national mental health advocacy programs and worked for several public interest lobbying organizations in Washington, D.C. while studying law at Georgetown University.